INTRODUCTION TO NEW TESTAMENT
TEXTUAL CRITICISM
Revised Edition

Introduction to New Testament Textual Criticism

Revised Edition

J. Harold Greenlee

© 1995 Hendrickson Publishers
P. O. Box 3473
Peabody, Massachusetts 01961–3473
All rights reserved
Printed in the United States of America

ISBN 1–56563–037–8

First Hendrickson Publishers' edition printed 1995

© 1964 Eerdmans Publishing Company
Assigned 1995 J. Harold Greenlee
Assigned 1995 Hendrickson Publishers

Library of Congress Cataloging-in-Publication Data

Greenlee, J. Harold (Jacob Harold), 1918–
   Introduction to New Testament textual criticism /
J. Harold Greenlee. — Rev. ed.
      p. cm.
   Includes bibliographical references.
   ISBN 1–56563–037–8
   1. Bible. N.T.—Criticism, Textual. I. Title.
BS2325.G67   1995
225.4′8—dc20   94-38503
                                                                CIP

To the memory of

WILLIAM DAVID TURKINGTON

First my respected professor, then my esteemed dean
and beloved colleague, who gave me my first instruction
in the intriguing field of New Testament textual criticism,
this book is sincerely dedicated.

CONTENTS

LIST OF FIGURES AND PLATES

FIGURES

PLATES

PREFACE

This book is a primer. It does not seek to make a contribution to the knowledge of those who are already scholars of New Testament texual criticism. The aim of this book is simply to present the facts and principles of New Testament texual criticism that are generally accepted. It will have fulfilled its purpose if it succeeds in presenting these facts and principles in a manner that will enable the beginning student to understand them and to begin to make his or her way in this intriguing and important field in which the rewards of careful labor are great.

I wish to acknowledge with thanks the courtesy of the University of Michigan, the Trustees of the British Museum, the Smithsonian Institution, and the Bibliothèque Nationale of Paris, for their kind permission to use photographs of manuscripts from their collection.

I wish to give a special word of appreciation to the officers of the Christian Research Foundation, by whom the manuscript of the present book was awarded a prize of five hundred dollars in 1961.

My thanks are due to my wife, who encouraged me to write this book; to Mrs. John J. Pawelski, who assisted with the typing; to the Rev. William B. Coker and the Rev. H. Bruce Wideman, who assisted with the index; and to Dr. Robert P. Markham, Prof. Allen Wikgren, Miss Karen Goodling, and to students in my classes in New Testament textual criticism in Asbury Theological Seminary and at Winona Lake School of Theology, who examined or used the book in manuscript form and helped to point out errors and to suggest improvements.

J. H. G.

PREFACE TO THE SECOND EDITION

The revisions in this second edition, other than minor changes, are principally in two areas:

I have stated the principles of internal evidence in what I believe is a more logical presentation than before, which has also meant re-ordering the discussion of internal evidence in discussing the variants.

The UBS Greek New Testament, which was only in preparation when the first edition of the present work was published, is now the basic referent text for the discussion of the variants in this edition. This has resulted in less dependence on the other editors and some improvements in the citation of witnesses for the variants discussed.

I wish to express my thanks to Professor William F. Warren for his helpful input and whose preparation of a Spanish translation of this book encouraged me to revise the English edition. In addition, Professor Bruce M. Metzger and Dr. Harold P. Scanlin provided invaluable information; for their help I am grateful.

JHG
Fort Myers, Florida
October 1994

Chapter 1

INTRODUCTION

A. DEFINITION

What did a book of the New Testament look like when it was first written? How were the books of the New Testament handed down through the centuries so as to reach us as we now know them? Can we safely conclude that the New Testament today accurately represents what the authors of these books originally wrote? These and related questions are considered in the study of the *textual criticism* of the New Testament.

Textual criticism is the study of copies of any written work of which the autograph (the original) is unknown, with the purpose of ascertaining the original text. Textual criticism is therefore not limited to the New Testament. It is a necessary study for almost any piece of literature which was written, and of which copies were made, before the invention of printing. The principles, moreover, are the same for the New Testament as for any other work, although there are additional factors, which will be discussed in due course, which modify the application of these principles in particular circumstances.

Textual criticism, which has sometimes been called "lower criticism," must be distinguished from literary criticism, or "higher criticism." While textual criticism seeks to determine the original wording of a document, literary criticism takes this original text and seeks to determine any sources which may underlie it. Textual criticism deals primarily with manuscripts;

literary criticism deals largely with elements such as style, vocabulary, and historical background.

B. Preliminary Comments

Only since the invention of printing a mere five centuries ago has it been easy to determine the original contents of a book. In our day we are able to take it for granted that the printed form of a book accurately represents the author's original manuscript (although minor errors appear even in printed books). We can also be certain that every copy of the same edition of a book will be exactly alike. Before the invention of printing, however—a period which includes three-fourths of the time the New Testament has been in existence—each copy of a document had to be made individually by hand. If a document was of any appreciable length it would be virtually certain that no two copies would be exactly alike and that no copy would be identical with the original.

If the original manuscript of a document is preserved, and is known, then of course textual criticism is not necessary for that document. Unfortunately, the originals of ancient literature, including the New Testament, have long since perished. Even if by some near-miracle one of these autographs should be discovered, it would have to be subjected to the principles of textual criticism in order to identify it as the original, and certainty might not even then be possible.

If copying a document by hand leads to *variants* (variations and errors in the text), then each subsequent copy will contain most of the variants of its "parent" copy plus some additional variants of its own. This means that a manuscript which is many copies removed from the original will normally contain more errors than one which is an immediate copy of the original or only a few copies removed. The difficulty is to know how many copies lie between a manuscript at hand and the original. For this reason, it is assumed that, in general, a later manuscript (e.g., one written in the tenth century) is probably separated from the original by more intervening copies than is an older manuscript (e.g., one written in the fourth century). There are of course exceptions to this rule. A manuscript copied in the twelfth century might be six copies removed from the first-century original, while a manuscript copied in the ninth century might be twenty copies removed from the original. Yet since it is generally impossible to tell how many copies lie between a given manuscript and its original, the age of a manuscript must be presumed to give some indication of the number of copies which separate it from the original. This tentative judgment must then be weighed against other evidence derived from an examination of the text of the manuscript to reach a final decision concerning the accuracy of the text of the manuscript.

The probability that the original text of a document has been preserved in part depends upon two factors concerning the manuscripts. In the first place, the shorter the interval of time between the original document and the date when the earliest available manuscript (or manuscripts) was written, the more likely it is that only a few copies intervene between this manuscript and the original and therefore the greater the probability that the text of this manuscript accurately reflects the text of the original. In the second place, the greater the number of available manuscripts the greater is the probability that all of the original text has been preserved accurately among them. At the same time, the greater the number of manuscripts the greater will be the number of variants and hence the greater the complications in determining the true text from among the variant readings of the manuscripts.

Ideally, a chart illustrating the successive copies made from an original document would resemble a "family tree" showing the descendants of one person, as illustrated in Fig. 1. In actual practice, however, any manuscript in this genealogy may have been copied from two different manuscripts or may include readings or variants introduced from manuscripts other than the "parent" copy, which may give a picture more nearly resembling Fig. 2. The implications of this factor will appear later.

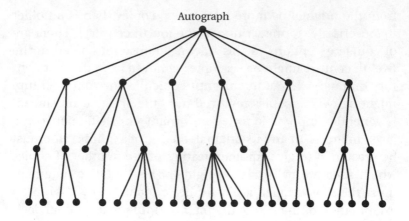

Figure 1

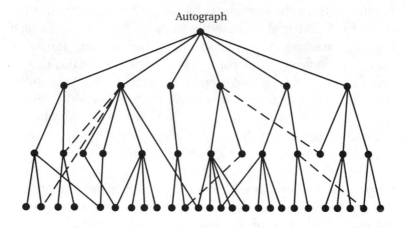

Figure 2

If all the copies which were made of a given original were extant (existing and known), it would no doubt be possible, in the ideal situation of Fig. 1, to place each MS (manuscript) in its proper place in the genealogy and to reconstruct the original with little hesitation. In actual fact, if many copies have been made of an original, as is notably the case with the New Testament, only a very few of these copies will be extant, and the original must be reached by less direct means. This is especially true since there are other complicating factors as well, including that indicated by Fig. 2.

If examining the available MSS (manuscripts) fails to indicate satisfactorily the original text of a certain word or phrase, a scholar may resort to an "educated guess" known as *conjectural emendation*. In the case of literature where there are only a few extant MSS this procedure may sometimes be necessary. When large number of MSS are available, as in the case of the New Testament, conecture is less often, if ever, necessary, and tends to become what Kenyon has called "a process precarious in the extreme, and seldom allowing anyone but the guesser to feel confidence in the truth of its results."[1]

C. The Place of the New Testament in Textual Criticism

Although the science of textual criticism is useful in the study of any piece of ancient literature, the most important branch of textual criticism is that which pertains to the New Testament. This is true for three interrelated reasons. In the first place, the NT is the most important piece of ancient literature. In the second place, the number of available MSS of the NT is overwhelmingly greater than those of any other work of ancient literature. In the third place, the earliest extant MSS of the NT were written much closer to the date of the original writing than is the case for almost any other piece of ancient literature.

The two latter points may be illustrated by a comparison. The plays of Aeschylus are known in some fifty MSS, the works of Sophocles in one hundred, the *Greek Anthology* and the *Annals* of Tacitus in one MS each, the poems of Catullus in three MSS of independent value, and there are a few hundred known

---

[1] Frederic G. Kenyon, *Handbook to the Textual Criticism of the New Testament*, 2d ed., 1926, p. 3.

MSS of works of Euripides, Cicero, Ovid, and Virgil. In the case of the NT, in sharp contrast, there are some 5000 extant MSS in Greek,[2] 8000 in Latin, and 1000 in other languages. As regards the time interval between the extant MSS and the autograph, the oldest known MSS of most of the Greek classical authors are dated a thousand years or more after the author's death. The time interval for the Latin authors is somewhat less, varying down to a minimum of three centuries in the case of Virgil. In the case of the NT, however, two of the most important MSS were written within 300 years after the NT was completed, and some virtually complete NT books as well as extensive fragmentary MSS of many parts of the NT date back to one century from the original writings.[3]

Since scholars accept as generally trustworthy the writings of the ancient classics, even though the earliest MSS were written so long after the original writings and the number of extant MSS is in many instances so small, it is clear that the reliability of the text of the NT is likewise assured.

D. THE AREA OF TEXTUAL CRITICISM

In the NT and in other ancient literature as well, there is no question concerning the reading of most of the words. Textual criticism needs to operate in only a limited portion of the text. When one is engaged in this study, and the number and importance of the variants are made the center of attention, it is well to remember that the main body of the text and its general sense are left untouched and that textual criticism engages in turning a magnifying glass upon some of the details.

---

[2]These MSS vary greatly in the extent of their contents. About 200 contain all or most of the NT, about 50 contain all except the Gospels. Approximately 1500 contain part or all of the Gospels alone. A great number contain only part of a book or a few verses.

[3]At the same time, it must be admitted that the scribes who copied the MSS of the classics were normally more careful about accuracy of details than were the earliest copyists of NT MSS.

E. The Priority of Textual Criticism

Textual criticism is the basic study for the accurate knowledge of any text. New Testament textual criticism, therefore, is the basic biblical study, a prerequisite to all other biblical and theological work. Interpretation, systematization, and application of the teachings of the NT cannot be done until textual criticism has done at least some of its work. It is therefore deserving of the acquaintance and attention of every serious student of the Bible.

Chapter 2

PALEOGRAPHY

A. MATERIALS FOR RECEIVING WRITING

1. Early Materials

A great variety of materials has been used to receive writing, even leaving out of consideration materials into which writing has been carved. In ancient times materials that were used to receive writing included such diverse items as the leaves and bark of trees, linen cloth, potsherds (broken pieces of pottery, designated "ostraca" when written on), walls of buildings (as in Herculaneum and Pompeii), metal, and wooden tablets with or without wax coating.

Waxed tablets were used in Greece and Rome from the earliest times. To make these tablets, a piece of wood was hollowed slightly, somewhat as a child's slate today, and the hollowed surface was coated with wax. Several such tablets might be fastened together, a leather thong through holes in the edge of the tablet forming the hinge. Such hinged tablets were doubtless the earliest form of the codex or modern book form. Waxed tablets were used not only for notebooks and temporary materials but also for correspondence and even for legal documents which needed to be preserved. In the latter, two tablets would be hinged face to face, which would protect the written surfaces. They could also be sealed against inspection, as in the case of a will. Waxed tablets were utilized over a period of sev-

eral centuries, long after the classical period. St. Augustine refers to some such tablets which he owned, made of ivory instead of wood. A few waxed tablets, some in Greek and some
in Latin, are extant. It is probably on such a tablet (πινακίδιον)
that Zechariah, father of John the Baptist, wrote his son's name
(Luke 1:63).

2. Papyrus

Papyrus, the writing material from whose name the word
"paper" is derived, was the common material for receiving
writing for many centuries. Papyrus (πάπυρος) was used in
Egypt from the earliest times, the oldest known fragment dating from about 2400 B.C. Papyrus as writing material was
taken for granted in Greece in the fifth century B.C. Inexpensive
and convenient, papyrus was used for both literary and non-
literary writings—letters, receipts, business matters, and other
purposes.

The papyrus plant is a reed which grew in swampy areas in
the delta of the Nile River and in a very few other places in the
Mediterranean world. The plant had a triangular-shaped stalk
with a tassel at the top, and grew to a height of from six to
twelve feet. The outer layers of the stalk were stripped off, leaving the pithy center. This center section was cut into thin strips
which were laid side by side. A second layer was then laid on
top of the first, crosswise of it (see Fig. 3). Paste may have been
used between the layers.

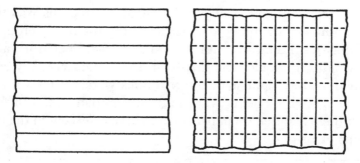

Figure 3

The sheets were then pounded to secure cohesion, left to dry, then smoothed with a piece of ivory or a shell. The pith of the papyrus was known as βίβλος or βύβλος (cf. "Bible," "bibliography"), and the resulting sheet as χάρτης (cf. "chart"). The latter Greek word occurs in 2 John 12.

The sheets usually ranged in size from 6 by 9 inches to 12 by 15 inches. The sheets were then overlapped slightly and pasted together, and were sold in rolls of twenty sheets. The best sheets were placed on the ends of the roll, since they would receive the greatest wear. Sometimes an extra strip would be placed at the beginning and end of the roll, which would give further reinforcement and would also aid in rolling. In Roman times, the first sheet of the unwritten roll was called the πρωτόκολλον ("first glued sheet"), and was commonly inscribed with the names of the officials who controlled the trade (cf. "protocol"). A book in roll form was called a βίβλος or βιβλίον from the papyrus strips. If a work comprised several rolls, one roll was called a τόμος, from τέμνω, "to cut" (cf. "tome").

Writing was done on the side of the roll on which the papyrus strips ran left and right, which was the inside of the roll. Writing would be more difficult on the side on which the strips were perpendicular to the line of writing, and only rarely would the back of the roll be written on. Such a roll written on both sides is an *opisthograph*, one of which may be referred to in Rev. 5:1. Papyrus later came to be used in the codex book-form, as is discussed below.

An important item of Egyptian export, papyrus was the common writing material especially until the third century,[1] for classical literarure until the sixth or seventh century, and even later for some documents. It is therefore virtually certain that the originals of the NT books were written on papyrus. Papyrus sheets were naturally perishable, and few documents written on papyrus have survived except in the dry sands of Egypt.

---

[1] Dates given are in the Christian era unless designated B.C.

3. Parchment or Vellum

The skins of animals (διφθέραι), in the form of tanned leather, were used to receive writing in very ancient times. They made strong and durable rolls. They were used by Persians, Hebrews, and Greeks, among others, but not much by the Egyptians because of their plentiful supply of papyrus. The oldest known specimens of leather scrolls date from about 1500 B.C. Leather rolls have continued to be used occasionally for the Hebrew OT down to modern times.

It was a later development, however, which brought animal skins into common use to receive writing. In this process, the skins were soaked in limewater, the hair was scraped off, and the skins were scraped and dried, then rubbed with chalk and pumice stone. The result was a fine, smooth writing surface of long-lasting quality. This material is known as *vellum* or *parchment*. Vellum is properly calfskin, but the term came to refer to other skins of the finer types as well, while parchment referred to ordinary skins; but the two terms are now used interchangeably. The term "parchment" derives from the name of the city of Pergamum, which was noted for its fine quality of this product.

It seems rather surprising that parchment was at first considered inferior to papyrus and was primarily used for notebooks, rough drafts, and other non-literary purposes. As time passed, perhaps partly because papyrus was unable to fill the increasing demands for writing material, and partly because of an increasing recognition of the superiority of parchment, papyrus was more and more displaced in general use. By the third or fourth century parchment was the common material for receiving writing, although papyrus, as has been said, continued to be used to some extent as late as the seventh century.

Only the very earliest NT MSS now in existence are on papyrus. Practically all of the MSS from the fourth to the fourteenth century are written on parchment. In 331 the Emperor Constantine ordered fifty copies of the Bible to be made on parchment for the churches of Constantinople. In 350, old and damaged papyrus volumes from the library of Pamphilus in

Caesarea were replaced by parchment copies. Indeed, the Christian church is given credit for the displacement of papyrus by parchment, when both tradition and the established book trade favored the continuance of the use of papyrus for literary writings. Thus papyrus is the traditional writing material for the pagan classics and parchment for the Christian writings.

4. Paper

Paper was invented by the Chinese—according to Chinese tradition, by one Tsai Lun, in A.D. 89. The oldest known specimens, from the fourth century, are paper made of hemp or flax. Paper became known to the Arabs about the eighth century and was introduced into the Western world at the time of the Crusades. The oldest extant paper MS of Europe is dated 1109. Paper began to be used in Europe for books in the twelfth century, rivaled parchment by the mid-fourteenth, and had virtually replaced parchment by the fifteenth century, shortly before the printing press brought about a revolution in the world of literature.

B. WRITING UTENSILS

1. Stilus

The common instrument for writing on the ancient waxed tablets was a stilus. Made of metal, ivory, or bone, the stilus had a point at one end for writing and a rounded knob at the other for making corrections.

2. Reed Pen

The earliest type of pen for use in writing on leather or papyrus was the reed pen (κάλαμος; see 3 John 13). The earliest known examples of reed pens were frayed at the ends like a brush. Pointed pens date from about the third century B.C. and were used at least to some extent through the Middle Ages and later. It is safe to assume that virtually all extant papyrus MSS, both of the NT and of other documents, were written with a reed pen. To make a reed pen, the reed stalk was dried, sharpened to a point on one end, and slit somewhat as a modern pen point is slit. Beautiful writing was possible with such pens.

3. Quill Pen

The quill pen is first mentioned much later than the reed pen. A quill would have been too firm for satisfactory writing on papyrus, but was probably introduced soon after parchment came into use. It largely supplanted the reed pen and became the ordinary pen for writing on parchment. The point of the quill was sharpened and slit for writing much as was the reed pen.

4. Other Implements

Ink used in ancient MSS was most commonly one of two kinds: ink made of lamp-black and gum dissolved in water, which produced very black writing; and ink made from nutgalls, which produced a fine rusty-brown color such as that in Codex B and Codex D. Red ink was sometimes used as were other colors, including purple, gold, and silver. Black ink is mentioned in 2 John 12 and 3 John 13.

The scribe would need some additional implements as well, including a knife for making a new pen, a whetstone for sharpening the knife, pumice stone for smoothing the parchment sheet and for sharpening the pen point, and a sponge for erasing and for wiping the pen point.

C. BOOK FORMS

1. Roll

The books (βιβλία) of the first century were papyrus rolls, the form which had been in use for centuries. A papyrus roll was commonly composed of twenty sheets glued together, but more sheets could be added or more than one roll glued together. The title of a work was usually given at the end, but a papyrus tag containing the title was also often attached to the top of the roll as an aid to the reader.

Columns of writing in a roll (or scroll) were ordinarily two to three inches wide, often without regard to the joining of the sheets. A narrow column would be desirable in a roll, since less of the roll would then have to be opened at one time. Margins between the columns were likewise narrow. The writing was always done so that the roll was used horizontally, not vertically. In Greek, Latin, and other languages in which writing proceeds from left to right, the roll would be unrolled from the right and rolled to the left. In a Hebrew roll the writing and the rolling would be in the opposite direction. Sticks or other types of rollers may sometimes have been used, but the roll could also simply be rolled on itself. When a writer or reader had completed a roll, it was re-rolled by holding the roll under the chin and rolling with both hands. Failure of a reader to re-roll a book would be considered a mark of laziness.

The roll form of book would involve obvious difficulties for reading through a work in several sittings, and especially would involve difficulties for reference purposes. There was even a proverb, "A great book, a great evil." This difficulty of reference became particularly acute in regard to the Christian scriptures. As a result, Christianity exercised the greatest single influence in bringing about the use of the codex book form and the displacement of the roll.

Several NT passages probably refer to papyrus rolls. In 2 Tim. 4:13, βιβλία and μεμβράνας may refer to papyrus rolls and parchment rolls or codices respectively, or possibly to leather rolls and parchment codices respectively. The "roll" of Isaiah, and the process of unrolling and re-rolling it, are referred to in Luke 4:17, 20. John's Gospel is referred to as a βιβλίον in John 20:30. Revelation 6:14 describes the sky as vanishing like a scroll which is rolled up (βιβλίον ἑλισσόμενον). The possible reference to an opisthograph, a roll written on both sides, in Rev. 5:1, has already been mentioned.

2. Codex

Ancient waxed tablets, fastened together by a thong hinge, furnished the model for the modern book form, although it was impractical to fasten together more than a very few tablets.

It was long thought that the change from the roll to the codex form of book coincided with the change from papyrus to parchment. The evidence makes it clear, however, that the codex was common while papyrus was still being used. There are now extant very extensive NT MSS and fragments on papyrus, some from as early as the second century, and not one can be clearly identified as a NT roll.

The codex seems to have been first used for notebooks or for an author's early drafts of a work, even when the final form was to be written on a roll. Its advantages for reading, and especially for reference, soon brought it into common use, especially for the NT. The secular classics continued to be copied on rolls until much later.

It has been said that when the codex first displaced the roll the narrow columns characteristic of the roll were carried over into the codex, with the columns gradually becoming wider for convenience in reading. Codex א, for example (4th cent.), has four columns to a page; Codex B (4th cent.), has three columns; Codex A (5th cent.), two columns, and Codex D (6th cent.), one column. Later MSS usually have one or two columns to the page. On the other hand, contrary evidence is found in the fact that the very earliest NT MSS, the papyri, show no such development, but have one wide column or two narrower columns to the page.

Codices are formed of quires (folded sheets). Occasionally a codex was made with only one folded sheet to a quire. At the other extreme was the book made of a single quire, with all the sheets of the book folded into one quire. This type would be unsatisfactory for all but the briefest books, as it would tend to fly open at the middle, open unevenly, and the center sheets would be smaller or would project beyond the outer sheets. The most common type of quire, however, was formed of four folded sheets, while quires of from three to six sheets are sometimes found. The quires of a given book would, of course, be uniform. In a papyrus quire the sheets would usually be placed so that vertical strips faced each other and horizontal strips faced each other. In parchment quires the hair side of a sheet would face a hair side, and the flesh side would face a flesh side. The quire itself would likewise be matched to adjacent quires.

New Testament MSS earlier than the fourth century are exclusively on papyrus; those from the fourth century and later are, with a few exceptions, on parchment.

A papyrus codex had one distinct disadvantage for the scribe in that on every alternate page the scribe was forced to write across the fibers. This disadvantage was not found in the papyrus roll, where the writing was done on one side only, nor in the parchment codex, where the difference in the surface of the flesh side and the hair side was much less noticeable.

Since the supply of parchment was not unlimited and since the sheets were quite durable, when a parchment codex was no longer wanted or became unusable the writing was sometimes scraped off and a new text written over it. Sometimes the quires would be turned upside down for the new text. Sometimes the sheets would be separated, cut through the fold, and folded again into sheets half the original size. Codex C is an example of the former and Codex Ξ of the latter. A MS thus rewritten is called a *palimpsest* (from πάλιν, "again," and ψάω, "I scrape"; see Plate 5). More than fifty Greek NT MSS of the tenth century and earlier are palimpsests.

In the past, attempts were sometimes made to recover the original text of palimpsest MSS by the use of chemical solutions; but this radical treatment sometimes damaged both the later text and the original. Codex C is one which has suffered in this manner. Other methods, including ultra-violet or infrared light, are now used, both for photography and (in the case of ultra-violet) for direct reading of the MS as well. Indeed, it is sometimes possible to read much of the original text, in spite of the later writing, with no aids other than good light, good eyes, and patience. This is possible because in preparing the sheets for rewriting it was apparently not considered necessary that the original text be completely obliterated, and even now it is often surprisingly visible.

D. HANDWRITING

1. Styles of Handwriting

a. Uncial. For many centuries two styles of Greek handwriting existed side by side, one for literary and the other for
non-literary writing. The literary hand is known as *uncial* (possibly from the Latin *uncialis,* "inch-high") or *majuscule.* Uncial
letters are derived from the stiff capital letters used in stone
inscriptions, but with their lines somewhat rounded and adapted
for facility in writing. Uncial letters are not connected to each
other. Texts are written with no division between words, although a system of syllable division is carefully observed at the
end of a line. The absence of spacing between words seems to
have been simply a convention, for if economy of space were important, the size of the letters in many MSS could have been
reduced.

In the earlier centuries uncial MSS were written with practically no accents, breathings, punctuation marks, or adorn-
ments. As time passed, the use of large and ornate initial letters
and other ornamentation, more elegant varieties of writing,
paragraph spacing, and punctuation and diacritical marks (accents and breathings) were introduced. A chronological display
of MSS would show a general evolution in these respects.[2] Manuscripts of the NT earlier than the tenth century are written in uncial letters.

b. Minuscule. Alongside the uncial or literary hand there
existed a style of writing used for non-literary materials
known as *cursive,* a Latin derivitive meaning "running." Cursive
letters are connected, but the handwriting is much less continuous than modern English handwriting. Cursive writing was

---

[2]See W. H. P. Hatch, *Principal Uncial Manuscripts,* or E. M. Thompson, *Introduction to Greek and Latin Palaeography,* pp. 201–16.
Thompson also (pp. 144–47) gives some representative alphabets for
the period of the fourth century B.C. through the second Christian
century.

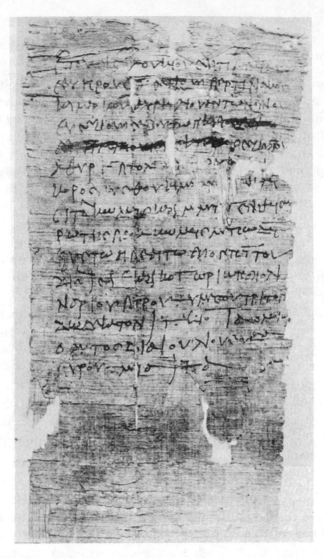

Plate 1

A receipt issued to Horion, son of Apolinarius, A.D. 207. Cursive
handwriting. The first four lines are ετους ιϛ Λουκιου Σεπτιμμιου /
Σεουηρου Ευσεβους Περτινακος / και Μαρκου Αυρηλιου Αντω-
νεινου / Ευσεβους Σεβαστων [   ] / . (Univ. of Mich. Inv. 2923,
P. Mich. VI, 398. Used by permission of the University of Michigan.)

used for personal correspondence, business and legal papers, and such matters (see Plate 1). It seems likely, therefore, that the originals of the letters of St. Paul were written in a cursive hand, since they were written as personal letters and not as formal literature. Almost as soon as they began to be copied, however, they would take on the character of literature and would be copied in the uncial hand of literature. If there were cursive MSS of some of the NT writings in the first century, none are known.

In the early part of the ninth century the cursive hand was somewhat modified and formalized into a *minuscule* or "small-letter" style deemed suitable for books and literature.[3] This made the writing of literary MSS more rapid than was possible with uncial letters. By the end of the tenth century this minuscule hand had displaced the uncial hand for literary purposes.

One of the earliest minuscule MSS of the Gospels is dated A.D. 835, which is also the earliest extant MS of the NT to contain a date.

Like the uncial MSS, the earliest minuscules were more carefully and simply written, while more ornamentation and sometimes less care in writing appear in the MSS of later centuries.[4]

Style of handwriting, then, provides a rather definite line of demarcation between two periods of NT MSS and the MSS of other literature as well, with uncial MSS coming from the tenth

---

[3] The terms "cursive" and "minuscule" are often used interchangeably. It is well, however, to retain the term "cursive" for the less-formal hand of personal notes and non-literary documents, and "minuscule" for the literary hand which was developed from the cursive, as Hatch, *Minuscule Manuscripts*, p. 3, indicates. There is a distinct difference between the two, as can be seen by comparing the cursive notes which a scribe sometimes added at the bottom of a page of a minuscule NT MS (e.g., Lect. 299), or by comparing a business document with a NT MS (e.g., Thompson, *Palaeography*, Facs. 41, p. 182, and Facs. 54, p. 224).

[4] See Hatch, *Minuscule Manuscripts*, or Thompson, *Palaeography*, pp. 150–83.

century and earlier and minuscule MSS from the tenth century and later.

Approximately nine-tenths of the extant Greek NT MSS are from the minuscule period.

2. Abbreviation

Properly speaking, abbreviation is a general term referring to the shortening of a word in writing. Abbreviation may take one of four common forms: contraction, in which part of the middle of the word is omitted, as in the English "Dr." for "Doctor"; suspension, in which the end of a word is omitted, as in "Oct." for "October"; ligatures, in which two or more letters are combined into one syllable, as "ff" and "fi" in some styles of modern type; and symbols, as "&" for "and."

a. *Contraction.* In NT MSS, abbreviation by contraction is limited to a definite group of fifteen special words. Since most of them relate to God and to sacred matters, they are commonly designated *nomina sacra,* "sacred names" (the singular, *nomen sacrum*). These words are as follows:[5]

θεός	θ̅ς̅	μήτηρ	μ̅η̅ρ̅
κύριος	κ̅ς̅	πατήρ	π̅η̅ρ̅
υἱός	υ̅ς̅	σώτηρ	σ̅η̅ρ̅
Ἰησοῦς	ι̅ς̅	ἄνθρωπος	α̅ν̅ο̅ς̅
Χριστός	χ̅ς̅	οὐρανός	ο̅υ̅ν̅ο̅ς̅
πνεῦμα	π̅ν̅α̅	Δαυίδ	δ̅α̅δ̅
σταυρός	σ̅τ̅ς̅	Ἰσραήλ	ι̅η̅λ̅
		Ἰερουσαλήμ	ι̅λ̅η̅μ̅

The divine names or titles seem first to have been contracted out of reverence, in an attempt to approximate the reverential

---

[5] The forms given are in the nominative case. The contracted form of other cases of these words would be analogous; e.g., π̅ρ̅ς̅ = πατρός, ο̅υ̅ν̅ο̅ν̅ = οὐρανόν.

treatment of the sacred name of God in Hebrew MSS. This principle was then extended to a few other words, all of which are associated with sacred matters. Thus, in marked distinction from other abbreviations, these contractions were not made for the purpose of saving space or labor. That this is true is seen in two related facts. In the first place, contraction as a type of abbreviation is distinctly limited to the MSS of the Bible and of Christian literature, and is virtually unknown in secular literature. In the second place, even in biblical MSS these very same words are often not contracted if they are used in any other than the specialized sense; e.g., πατήρ is usually contracted only when it refers to God, and ἄνθρωπος only in such references as "the Son of Man" as a title of Jesus. There are, of course, exceptions to this general principle.

b. Suspension. Suspension is the ordinary type of abbreviation, used to save time or space, and used especially at the end of a line. Suspension is indicated in one of several ways:

(i) The first letter only may be written, with a characteristic mark to show suspension: e.g., ὑ (υἱός), *κϑ* (καί).

(ii) The first part of the word may be written, with a horizontal line above the last letter to indicate suspension: e.g., τελ̄ (τέλος).

(iii) In NT uncial MSS, suspension is confined almost entirely to the omission of a final ν at the end of a line, indicated by a horizontal line above and following the last written letter: e.g., πολῑ (πόλιν).

(iv) The first part of the word may be written with the last written letter or letters above the line and smaller: e.g., τε^λ (τέλος), τ^εκ (τέκνα).

c. Ligatures. Ligatures are not common in uncial MSS. In minuscule MSS the line cannot always be carefully drawn between ligatures and two connected letters, but the following may be suggested:

&ɣ (εγ) ᓂ (εσ) ᕬ (ευρ) ४ (ου) ୟ (στ).

d. Symbols. Few abbreviation symbols are found in the uncial MSS. In minuscule MSS they are found more often in later than in earlier MSS. The following are some examples:[6] Ⅴ = και, α͞υ͞τ = αυτων, α͞υ͞τ = αυτοις, τ`` = -τον, ι͵ = -ιον, ι͡ = -ιαν, μ′ = μου, π͞λ· = -πεν, ζ″ = -ζειν.

A summary of the significant paleographical features of Greek NT MSS from the first century down to the age of printing may be seen in the chart on p. 23.

---

[6] Most of the examples given are found in Lect. 299, the later text written over the palimpsest Codex Ξ. Thompson, *Palaeography,* pp. 80–84, gives an extensive list of symbols.

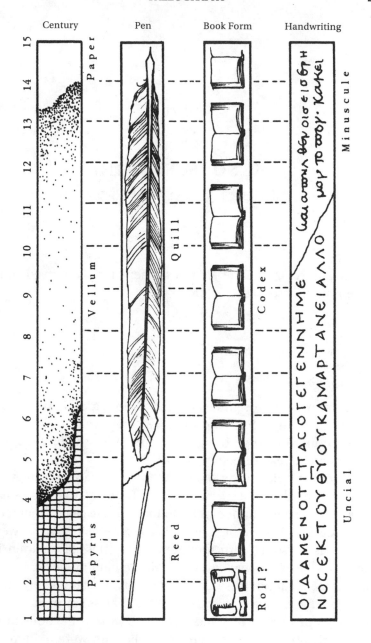

Figure 4

Chapter 3

THE SOURCES OF THE
NEW TESTAMENT TEXT

Our knowledge of the New Testament text is derived from three principal sources.

A. GREEK MANUSCRIPTS

1. Autographs

The autographs (originals) of the NT books are a hypothetical source only, since none are extant. If they were available, NT textual criticism would be unnecessary, since the original text could then be read directly.

The autographs of the NT books were probably on papyrus and could hardly have survived except possibly in the dry sand of Egypt or in conditions similar to those in the caves where the Dead Sea Scrolls have been found. The NT epistles which were written as personal correspondence were possibly written in the non-literary cursive hand, and the remaining books in un-cial letters. It cannot be said with certainty what book form was used for the autographs. It is possible that some of St. Paul's letters, as private correspondence, were written in codex form and those which were written for publication were written on rolls. It has been estimated that the short epistles could have been written on one papyrus sheet, while Matthew would have required a papyrus roll thirty feet long.

2. Papyri

The earliest extant witnesses to the NT text are the papyrus MSS. At least 98 papyrus MSS are now known and identified. Their contents vary from a scrap containing three or four verses to a MS originally containing the Gospels and Acts, and others containing extensive parts of the Pauline epistles, Catholic Epistles, and Revelation. Most of the papyri come from the second through the fourth centuries, although some are later.

The first discovery of papyrus MSS in modern times was in 1778 in the Fayum province of Egypt. More were found from time to time, but their significance was long overlooked and some were destroyed or burned. It was not until near the end of the nineteenth century that significant quantities of papyrus MSS began to come to light by discovery and publication, which caused scholars to realize that these papyrus MSS were veritable treasures. Most of the papyri are non-literary documents—business receipts, personal letters, deeds, and such matters—and are important for the light which they shed on customs, ideas, culture, and the language of the times. Other papyrus MSS contain literary works, including both secular classics and the Bible.

In designating MSS of the Greek NT, the papyri are indicated by a capital or gothic capital letter followed by a superscript numeral (e.g., $\mathfrak{P}^{53}$). This is the designation used in NT textual criticism. Of course, when these MSS are housed in a library they usually have a local library catalog number as well.

Among the most important papyri are the following:

$\mathfrak{P}^{45}$, $\mathfrak{P}^{46}$, $\mathfrak{P}^{47}$, known as the Chester Beatty papyri, contain much of the Gospels and Acts, Pauline epistles, and Revelation respectively, and date from the third century. Most of these three MSS are in the Chester Beatty collection in Dublin, although part of $\mathfrak{P}^{45}$ is in Vienna and part of $\mathfrak{P}^{46}$ is owned by the University of Michigan.

$\mathfrak{P}^{52}$, in the John Rylands Library of Manchester, England, is a small fragment containing parts of four verses of John 18. This

Plate 2

$\mathfrak{P}^{37}$, Matthew 26:19–52. 3d century, Western text. (Univ. of Mich. Inv. 1570, P. Mich. III, 137. Used by permission of the University of Michigan.)

is the oldest known fragment of the NT, dating from the first half of the second century. It is written on both sides, indicating that it is from a codex, not a roll.

$\mathfrak{P}^{66}$, $\mathfrak{P}^{72}$, $\mathfrak{P}^{74}$, and $\mathfrak{P}^{75}$ are part of an extensive papyrus collection of the Bodmer Library in Geneva, Switzerland. This collection, which includes both Greek and Coptic as well as secular and sacred texts, has been in process of publication since 1954. The biblical texts of this collection rival or exceed the Chester Beatty papyri in importance. The source of these papyri has not been made known.

$\mathfrak{P}^{66}$ (Bodmer Papyrus II) contains most of the Gospel of John and dates from ca. A.D. 200.

$\mathfrak{P}^{72}$ contains Jude (Papyrus Bodmer VII) and the epistles of Peter (Papyrus Bodmer VIII), together with Psalms 33 and 34 in Greek (Papyrus Bodmer IX), and dates from the third century.

$\mathfrak{P}^{74}$ (Papyrus Bodmer XVII) contains Acts virtually complete and the Catholic Epistles in fragmentary form. Dating from the seventh century, it is one of the latest extant Greek NT papyri, but contains a good form of text.

$\mathfrak{P}^{75}$ contains most of Luke (Papyrus Bodmer XIV) and of John (Papyrus Bodmer XV) from the early third century.

3. Uncial Manuscripts

Although the papyrus MSS are likewise written in uncial letters, the term *uncial MSS* ordinarily designates those on parchment, hence MSS of the fourth through the tenth centuries. At least 300 uncial MSS are known, varying from small fragments or a few sheets to nearly complete New Testaments or Bibles.

The change from the roll to the codex book form made it feasible to have more than one of the longer NT books in one volume. With the change from papyrus to the stronger parchment it became possible to have the complete NT in one volume by the use of more and larger sheets. The transition to parchment, moreover, came not long before Christianity attained official recognition in the Roman Empire under the Emperor Constantine about 325, after which time the Scriptures could be copied and distributed openly and officially.

Generally speaking, the uncial MSS, especially the earlier ones, are the most dependable group of witnesses to the NT text. While most of the papyri are earlier, some of them show evidence of having been copied without professional care, which lessens their dependability especially in matters of detail.

The earliest uncials are simple and unadorned, with an increasing amount of ornamentation observable in MSS from subsequent centuries.

Uncial MSS are designated in two ways, by letter and by number. From the beginning of the eighteenth century capital letters were used. When the number of MSS exceeded the number of letters in the English alphabet, capital letters of the Greek alphabet that differed from English letters were used. When Tischendorf discovered the famous Codex Sinaiticus he felt that it was too significant to be identified by the next available letter and instead designated it by the first letter of the Hebrew alphabet, Codex Aleph (א). The number of MSS, however, increased even beyond the limits of these two alphabets. Consequently, about 1890 Caspar René Gregory devised a new system whereby all uncial MSS are now designated by a numeral with a zero prefixed—e.g., 01, 023, 0168. Most of those which have both a letter and a numeral designation are still better known by their letter, however.

The numeral system has clarified another complication of the previous systems. Since very few MSS contained the entire NT, it had become the practice to assign the same letter designation to more than one MS if their contents did not overlap. For example, one MS containing the Gospels and Acts was designated by the letter D (Codex Bezae), and a different MS containing the Pauline epistles but not the Gospels or Acts was designated Codex D2 or D^Paul (Codex Claromontanus). In the numeral system, on the other hand, each MS has a different numeral: Codex D is 05, Codex D2 is 06; Codex S of the Gospels is 028, Codex S of Acts is 049.

Some of the more important uncial MSS: Codex א (01), also known as Codex Sinaiticus, written in the fourth century; it is

Plate 3

Mark 1:1–35 of Codex Sinaiticus (ℵ, 01), 4th century. (Used by permission of the Trustees of the British Museum.)

one of the two most famous uncial MSS and is on permanent display in the British Museum in London. It contains the complete NT (with part of the OT plus some sub-apostolic Christian writings). The writing is neat and unadorned, with four columns of text to the page. The discovery of this MS in the Monastery of St. Catherine on Mt. Sinai by the great scholar, Constantin von Tischendorf, is a fascinating story. Tischendorf took the MS from Mt. Sinai to Russia in 1859, and it was purchased from Russia by the British government in 1933 for £100,000.

Codex A (02), or Codex Alexandrinus, written in the fifth century, is displayed by the side of Codex ℵ in the British Museum. This MS contains the complete NT except for most of Matthew and part of John and 2 Corinthians. It also contains the OT and some other writings. This MS has been used in modern times by textual scholars longer than any other uncial MS. It has been in England since 1627. Its text is written two columns to the page in a beautiful and relatively unadorned style.

Codex B (03), or Codex Vaticanus, is the other of the two most famous uncial MSS. It is one of the treasures of the Vatican Library, where it has rested since 1481 or earlier. Written in the fourth century, it is probably the best single MS of the NT. Its text has been fully available to textual scholars only within the past century. The writing is in a beautiful but simple uncial hand, three columns to the page. The NT lacks part of Hebrews, the Pastoral Epistles, and Revelation. It also contains most of the OT.

Codex C (04), also known as Codex Ephraemi Rescriptus, is a palimpsest whose later text is some treatises of St. Ephraem, from which the MS received its name. It is located in the National Library of Paris. Its contents cover the NT, but in fragmentary form with many leaves missing. (The OT is similarly included.) The MS dates from the fifth century. The writing is one column to the page. The pages are now somewhat defaced, due to the use of chemicals in earlier attempts to restore the original writing. Tischendorf published the text of this MS in 1843 and 1845. In 1958 Robert Lyon re-read the NT, making some corrections in Tischendorf's work.

Plate 4

An uncial MS, Codex W (032), the Freer Gospels, written in the 5th century. The page shown contains Mark 1:1–7. (Used by permission of the Smithsonian Institution, Freer Gallery of Art.)

Plate 5

Folio 110 r. (2 Cor 1:1–8) of Codex 0209, a fragmentary uncial palimpsest of the 7th century, comprising the earlier (erased) text of eight folios of Mich. MS 8. The title of the epistle is visible at the top left. The first three lines of the left-hand column, and one line in the lower half of the right-hand column, are in red ink and are therefore more clearly visible than is the rest of the uncial text. The later (upper) text is a 14th-century Christian service book in a minuscule hand. (Used by permission of the University of Michigan.)

Codex D (05), or Codex Bezae, is a sixth-century MS of the Gospels and Acts, with Greek and Latin on facing pages. The MS is located in the Cambridge University Library and has been in England since it was brought from a monastery in France in 1581. Its text is written one column to the page, with lines of greatly differing length.

Codex W (032), or Codex Washingtonensis (or Freerianus), is a MS containing the four Gospels in the order Matthew, John, Luke, Mark. One of the few uncial MSS located in the United States, it was purchased in Egypt in 1906 by Mr. C. L. Freer and is now in the Freer Art Gallery of the Smithsonian Institution in Washington. It dates possibly from the fifth century. Its text is one column to the page.

4. Minuscule Manuscripts

By far the largest group of Greek NT MSS are those written in minuscule handwriting, thus dating from the ninth century and later. Most are on parchment; the few on paper are generally so late as to be of little importance to textual criticism. As already stated, the minuscule hand was developed in the ninth century, and practically every MS written after the tenth century is a minuscule.

Being later than the uncials, most of the minuscules may be assumed to have an inferior text. This, however, is not always true. A twelfth-century minuscule, for example, might be only half as many copies removed from the autograph as an eighth-century uncial and might also have an ancestry of more accurate copying.

As in the case of the uncials, the relative date of minuscule MSS can be observed to some extent by the presence of more ornamentation and a growing carelessness of writing in the later minuscules.

The minuscule MSS are designated by numerals (e.g., Codex 13, Codex 1525), the list at present extending to approximately 2800. Manuscripts' contents vary from one or two pages to the complete NT. In previous numbering systems, as in the case of the uncials, the same number was often assigned to two

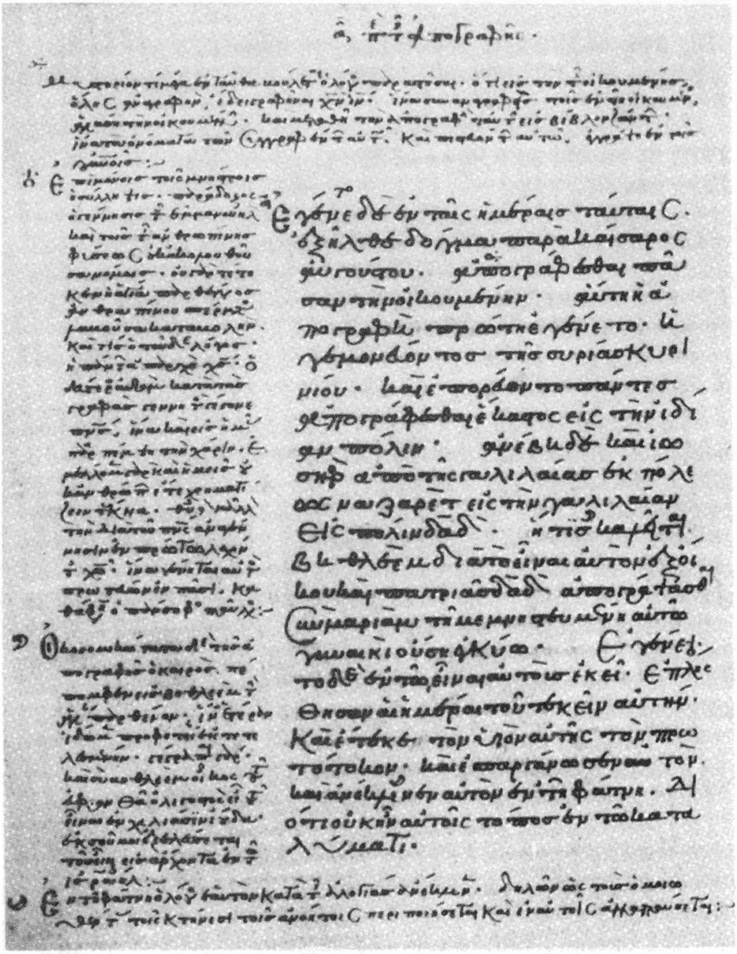

Plate 6

A minuscule MS, Codex 747, written in A.D. 1164. This MS contains the biblical text, with the smaller handwriting comprising a catena (excerpts from writings of various Fathers). Symbols within the biblical text corresponding to the symbols at the beginning of each section of the catena indicate the scripture passage to which each section of the catena refers. The page shown contains Luke 2:1–7. (Used by permission of the Bibliothèque Nationale, Paris.)

different MSS if their contents did not overlap. This older numeration is still met with at times and must be transferred into the present Gregory designations.

Some of the more important minuscule MSS may be noted:

Codex 1 is a twelfth-century MS located in Basel, Switzerland. It is noteworthy as one of the MSS used by Erasmus to prepare the first published Greek New Testament. The designation "Family 1" (f^1) is given to a group of minuscule MSS whose text is very similar to that of Codex 1: 118, 131, 209, 1582, and some others.

Codex 13, written in the thirteenth century, is in the National Library of Paris. "Family 13" (f^{13}), which includes Codices 13, 69, 124, 346, 543, and a few others, is likewise a closely related group of MSS. This family of MSS, in turn, is closely related to Family 1.

Codex 33, a tenth-century MS in the National Library of Paris, is known as "Queen of the Cursives" because of its reliable text.

Codex 565, from the tenth century, is in the Public Library of St. Petersburg, Russia. One of the most beautiful of all Greek NT MSS, it was written in gold letters on purple vellum, perhaps for the Empress Theodora. Accordingly, it is known as Codex Imperatricis Theodorae.

5. Lectionaries

The second largest group of NT MSS, and by far the most neglected in the past, are the lectionaries. These are MSS in which the Scriptures are written, not in ordinary sequence, but in sections arranged in units for reading in church services. In very ancient times certain scripture passages were designated as the reading for each day of the year and for special services and days. The lectionary MSS were then written to follow the sequence of readings, with the day and the week generally indicated at the beginning of each lection. Each daily reading (with few exceptions) is introduced by one of six set phrases:[1]

---

[1]Accents and breathings will be commonly omitted when variant readings are quoted unless they are necessary to the meaning or enter into the variant.

(i) τω καιρω εκεινω

(ii) ειπεν ο κυριος τοις εαυτου μαθηταις

(iii) ειπεν ο κυριος προς τους εληλυθοτας προς αυτον
Ιουδαιους

(iv) ειπεν ο κυριος προς τους πεπιστευκοτας αυτω Ιουδαιους

(v) ειπεν ο κυριος

(vi) ειπεν ο κυριος την παραβολην ταυτην

Minor adjustments in the NT words which immediately follow the opening phrase are also sometimes made: substitution of a noun for a pronoun, dropping of a conjunction, etc. Some NT passages appear in more than one lection during the year.

Some lectionaries contain the full daily set of lessons, while others contain only the Saturday and Sunday lessons. A lectionary containing lessons from the Gospels is called an "evangelistarion"; one containing lessons from the epistles is called an "apostolicon."

Some 2000 lectionary MSS are extant. As with the straight-text MSS, they range from fragments to complete MSS. Roughly one-fourth to one-third of these are of the epistles, seventy-five are combined Gospels and epistles, and the rest are Gospels.

The earliest lectionary fragments are from the sixth century, while complete MSS date from the eighth century and later. A considerable number of lectionary MSS are uncials, dating from the tenth century and earlier. A far greater number, of course, are minuscules.

Lectionaries are designated by a numeral preceded by the letter *l* in italics or by the abbreviation "Lect." (e.g., *l* 225, Lect. 225).

B. VERSIONS

Ancient literature was rarely translated into another language. In the occasional instances in which it was done, the resulting translation was in most cases of little use in determining the exact text of the original. When, therefore, the Hebrew OT was translated into Greek about the second century B.C., it stood virtually unique in literature.

The Christian faith is in its very nature a missionary religion. As the Christian message was carried abroad, the books of the NT were not only taken along but were also translated into the languages of the peoples to whom the message was given. Indeed, the NT books were first translated shortly after they were written. Both in the number of ancient translations or versions made and in their importance for study of the text the NT has no equal in literature.

In NT textual criticism the importance of a version is not, of course, in the version as an end in itself, but rather in the indications which the versions give of the Greek text from which they were first translated. With this in mind, there are certain preliminary considerations which must precede the use of a version for textual criticism:

(a) The original MS of the version is not extant, and the version is known only through copies more or less remote from the original text of the version. The principles of textual criticism must therefore be applied to the existing MSS of the version in order to determine as nearly as possible the exact original wording. This postulated original form of the version may then be studied in an attempt to decide the Greek text from which it was translated. For this purpose, a good literary translation might be of less value than one which translated the Greek forms so closely that it is inferior as a version.

(b) Inherent differences between the two languages must be taken into consideration. For example, since Latin has no definite article the Latin versions could not help in deciding between two readings such as πλοῖον and τὸ πλοῖον. Likewise a question of alternative word order in Greek could not be decided with the help of a version in which an obligatory word order is involved.

The place in which a version was made and the approximate date at which it was made are often known within certain limits. To the extent, then, to which the original form of the version can be determined, and consequently the Greek text from which the version was translated, the version sheds light upon the form of the Greek text which was in use at that period and in that geographical region.

A number of the ancient versions are of significance in NT textual criticism. The text of some of these has been studied with a view to identifying the MSS and text-types to which the version is related. Much work in this area, however, remains to be done.

1. Latin

a. Old Latin (Itala). Although Latin was the official language of the Roman Empire, Greek was the common language and continued to be so until about the third century. There was nevertheless an early need for a Latin NT, and this translation was made before the second century had passed. Thirty or more MSS of the Old Latin are known; the oldest, Codex Vercellensis (Codex a), dates from the fourth century. No single MS of the Itala contains the entire NT, but most of the NT is preserved in one or another of the MSS. Official designations for MSS of the Itala are lower-case letters—g, k, ff, etc.—and the version itself is abbreviated as OL, It (e.g., It^k), etc.

There is a good deal of uncertainty as to whether the Itala represents one or several translations, due to the great variety of readings in the MSS. The Latin of the Itala tends to be colloquial and unsophisticated, indicating that it had its source among the common people. Although the Itala was officially superseded by the Vulgate, the Itala seems to have been copied and used to some extent until the ninth century or later.

b. Vulgate. As time passed, especially after Christianity attained official status in the Roman Empire, the great variety of texts within the Itala became increasingly intolerable. Finally in 382 Pope Damasus commissioned Jerome, his advisor and the outstanding biblical scholar of his day, to undertake a revision of the Latin Bible, standardizing it by the "true Greek text." Although biblical studies were his life's work, Jerome accepted the assignment with reluctance, anticipating that his work would be judged harshly by the ignorant. He published the Gospels in 384, apparently making changes in the text only where he felt it was absolutely necessary. It is not clear how much of the rest of the NT is the work of Jerome and how much was done by other scholars, but at any event the entire NT was eventually completed. This version became the official Bible of the Latin church and remains today the Roman Catholic Bible. This version is designated the Vulgate, which identifies it as the "common" or "usual" version.[2]

No less than 8000 MSS of the Vulgate are now known, or many more than all the known Greek NT MSS. This suggests that the Vulgate Bible was the most frequently copied book of all ancient literature. Some of the more important MSS of the Vulgate are cited individually in NT critical apparatuses and are designed by abbreviations such as *am, for, tol, demid,* etc.

2. Syriac

a. The Diatessaron. Syriac, a language closely related to the Aramaic spoken by Jesus and his disciples, was spoken in countries neighboring Palestine. At least part of the NT may have been translated into Syriac as soon as or before the Old Latin version appeared. There seem to be indications that the first NT material in Syriac was a Gospel harmony by Tatian, composed about 160, in which the four Gospels were combined into one continuous account known as the Diatessaron (i.e., "through the Four"). Very little is known of this work except indirectly and by inference. It is not even certain whether the Diatessaron was originally composed in Syriac or was translated from a Greek original. No MSS are known which can be identified with Tatian's Diatessaron, but there are a very few MSS of similar harmonies in other languages which scholars have attempted to relate to some extent to Tatian's work. A

---

[2]The term "Vulgate" alone always refers to the Latin Vulgate; but "Vulgate" is also sometimes used together with the name of another version to refer to the commonly used form of that version—e.g., the "Armenian Vulgate."

fourteen-line fragment in Greek, dating from the third century, discovered at Dura in 1933, may be evidence that the Diatessaron was composed in Greek.

b. The Old Syriac. Probably subsequent to the appearance of Tatian's Diatessaron in Syriac, but likely by the end of the second century or the beginning of the third, the four Gospels (and perhaps more of the NT) were translated into Syriac. This version survives in two MSS of the Gospels which were discovered in Egypt in 1842 and at Mt. Sinai in 1892. The former, a fifth-century MS, was discovered by William Cureton and is known as the Curetonian Syriac. The latter, a palimpsest from the fourth or early fifth century, was discovered by Mrs. A. S. Lewis and Mrs. A. D. Gibson, English twin sisters, in the same monastery in which Tischendorf had earlier discovered Codex ℵ, and is known as the Sinaitic Syriac.

c. The Peshitta. The Syriac version which is still the standard Syriac text is the Peshitta (or Peshitto), meaning "simple." It apparently dates from the beginning of the fifth century or earlier. Rabbula, bishop of Edessa (consecrated in 411), has been credited with making this translation, but this conclusion is not universally accepted.

The Peshitta contained all of the NT books except 2 Peter, 2 and 3 John, Jude, and Revelation. These were omitted because they were not recognized as canonical by the Syrian church.[3] The Peshitta is known in 350 MSS or more, the oldest dating from the fifth century.

d. Philoxenian Syriac. In 508 a new Syriac NT was completed, including the books which were omitted from the Peshitta. This version was prepared for Philoxenus, bishop of Maburg in Syria, by Polycarp. One MS containing 2 Peter, 2 and 3 John, and Jude is known, and one MS of Revelation. It is not certain how

---

[3]In modern printed texts of the Peshitta the four omitted Catholic Epistles have been supplied from the Philoxenian Syriac and Revelation from the Harkleian.

much of the remaining NT books is extant, due to the unsettled question of the relationship between the Philoxenian and the Harkleian versions. As for the character of the Philoxenian, Kenyon refers to it as "written in free and idiomatic Syriac, being the most literary in form of all the translations of the New Testament into this language,"[4] while other scholars refer to it as being a more literal rendering of the Greek than was the Peshitta.[5]

e. Harkleian Syriac. In 616 Thomas of Harkel completed a work which has been known as the Harkleian (or Harclean) version. The question has been much disputed, however, as to whether Thomas simply added an extensive set of marginal alternate readings to the Philoxenian or whether he revised the Philoxenian rather thoroughly and added marginal readings which he thought were worthy of consideration as alternatives. The lack of a complete NT MS which can be identified definitely as the Philoxenian has, of course, hindered the solution of this problem. Those who maintain that the Harkleian is a distinct version state that it is distinguished as being so literal a rendering of the Greek that it violates Syriac idiom and style. It is the marginal readings of the Harkleian—which, of course, are unquestioned—which have been more used in textual criticism than the version itself. This version exists in about fifty MSS, from the eighth century and later.

f. Palestinian Syriac. The date of origin of the Palestinian Syriac version is unknown, but probably the fifth century would be a reasonable estimate. This version is unique in its present position in that it is known almost solely from lectionary MSS, with only fragments of MSS of continous text extant. Three lectionaries are known, dating from the eleventh and twelfth centuries. They follow closely the pattern of Greek lectionaries

---

[4]Kenyon, *Handbook*, p. 165.
[5]E.g., Vaganay, *Introduction to Textual Criticism of the New Testament*, p. 135; Souter, *Text and Canon of the New Testament*, 1.61; and Vööbus, *Early Versions of the New Testament*, pp. 116–17.

and suggest that this version may be a direct translation from Greek lectionaries into a Syriac lectionary.

Reference has at times been made to a so-called Karkaphensian Syriac version. This material is not a version, however, but simply a collection of Syriac texts accompanied by notes on orthography and pronunciation.

3. Coptic (Egyptian)

Although Greek was known and used in Egypt, there would naturally arise, before long, a need for the NT in the native language. In the second century, or possibly slightly earlier, an alphabet using Greek letters with certain modifications was developed for Egypt. This system of writing came to be called Coptic, and was distinct both from the ancient hieroglyphics and the demotic writing of everyday life which had been in use. The Bible was subsequently translated into several dialects of Coptic.

a. Sahidic. The Coptic dialect of southern or Upper Egypt is Sahidic. The Sahidic NT probably originated about the third century. Virtually the entire NT in this dialect is known from extant MSS, which include complete codices and many fragments from the fourth century and later.

b. Bohairic. Bohairic, the Coptic dialect of northern or Lower Egypt, was the most literary of the dialects. Within its area was Alexandria, the literary capital of Egypt. Bohairic eventually became the accepted dialect of the Coptic church and superseded the other dialects. Until recently, the earliest of the approximately 100 known Bohairic NT MSS were from the ninth century and later, and some scholars had suggested that the Bohairic NT originated no earlier than the seventh or eighth century. Yet it would seem strange if the dialect of Alexandria was without a NT for centuries after other dialects had the Scriptures. Moreover, the climate of northern Egypt is much less suitable for the preservation of MSS than are the dry sands of the south. The possibility of a late date was finally ruled out by the publication in 1958 of a papyrus of John in Bohairic

(Papyrus Bodmer III), which the editor, Rodolphe Kasser, dates in the fourth century, thus setting a date prior to which the Bohairic NT must have originated.

c. *Middle Egyptian dialects.* Between the regions of northern and southern Egypt there developed other dialects of Coptic, including Fayumic, Achmimic, and sub-Achmimic. Most of John is extant in Fayumic and sub-Achmimic. The Achmimic material includes a small part of John, the epistles of James and Jude, and fragments of Matthew and Luke from the fourth or fifth century.

4. Armenian

The NT seems to have been translated into the Armenian language in the early part of the fifth century under the sponsorship of the Patriarch Sahak, with most of the actual work being done by a monk Mesrop, who likewise was responsible for the Armenian alphabet. The Armenian version was translated either from the Syriac, in a form resembling the Old Syriac, or directly from the Greek. A revision appeared, perhaps based upon "trustworthy Greek codices" which tradition says were brought from Constantinople following the Synod of Ephesus in 431. This revised version, which became dominant over the Old Armenian at least by the eighth century, is the dominant Armenian text still in use. It is considered a beautiful and accurate translation of the Greek text. Manuscripts of the Armenian version are quite numerous, but only one is as old as the ninth century. Most of the MSS therefore contain the revised rather than the earlier version.

5. Georgian

The Christian message was known in Georgia, the mountainous area between the Black and Caspian Seas, in the fourth century. The NT was translated into Georgian by about the middle of the fifth century, using an alphabet which tradition credits to the same Mesrop who is said to have developed the Armenian alphabet. Although a number of scholars formerly held that the Georgian was made directly from the Greek, it seems more likely that it was made from the Armenian version, to which it has numerous affinities. The version was later revised, perhaps more than once and to varying degrees, with a final standardizing revision by or shortly before the eleventh century, which produced the text still in use. Many MSS of the Georgian version are known, including some lectionary material, dating from the end of the ninth century and later.

6. Ethiopic

Although the book of Acts records the conversion of an Ethiopian official, little is known concerning Christianity in Ethiopia until some centuries later. This makes it difficult to answer questions concerning the origin of the Ethiopic NT. Scholars have assigned it to dates as early as the second century and as late as the fourteenth. The version has been said to follow the Greek text slavishly at times, and it has been said to have been translated from the Syriac. Although more than 100 MSS are known, none is from earlier than the thirteenth century. Tentatively it may be suggested that the Ethiopic version was originally made from Syriac, although possibly from Greek, and that it originated between the fourth and seventh centuries. During the fourteenth century a revision was evidently made to bring the text more nearly into agreement with Arabic MSS of the NT known in Alexandria.

7. Gothic

It is not clear at what date the Christian faith was first introduced to the Gothic tribes who lived in the regions of the Danube River. The translation of the NT into Gothic, however, is attributed quite certainly by most scholars to Ulfilas, who was made bishop of the Goths in 348. Ulfilas is also given credit by some for the invention of the Gothic alphabet; but if he did make a contribution in this area it appears more likely that it was limited to refinements of an already existing alphabet. Much of the translation may have been done after Ulfilas and his followers were expelled by the king of the Goths and took refuge within the borders of the Roman Empire.

The Gothic version survives in about six MSS, all dating from the fifth and sixth centuries. All but one are fragmentary palimpsests. The remaining one, Codex Argenteus, preserved in the University Library at Uppsala, Sweden, contains about half of the Gospels written in silver letters (hence its name) on purple vellum.

8. Arabic

It is impossible to say how many translations of the NT into Arabic have been made, but it is clear that they have been numerous. The earliest was perhaps translated from Syriac, possibly the Old Syriac, near the time of the rise of Islam in the seventh century, but the date is by no means certain. Other translations or revisions were made or corrected from the Peshitta, Greek, Sahidic, Bohairic, Old Latin, and Vulgate. One group of MSS contains a text written in rhymed prose in the style of the Qur'an. Present-day printed Arabic Gospels are based upon a thirteenth-century version which was translated primarily from Bohairic with additions from Greek and Syriac. The extant MSS of the Arabic version are numerous, dating from the ninth century and later; but the value of the version in textual criticism is rather limited.

9. Persian

The Gospels in Persian are known from one fourteenth-century MS of a version translated from Syriac and from a later version translated from Greek. The dates of the origin of these versions is unknown, and they are little used in NT textual criticism.

10. Slavonic

The Slavonic version is credited to two brothers, Cyril and Methodius, who were missionaries to the Slavs of Bulgaria in the ninth century. Cyril is likewise credited with having invented the Slavic alphabet, and one form of the alphabet is called Cyrillic in his honor. Most of the known MSS are lectionaries, and the version may first have existed in lectionary form.

11. Frankish

One fragmentary eighth-century MS preserves parts of Matthew in Frankish, a language of west-central Europe, with Frankish and Latin on facing pages.

C. PATRISTIC QUOTATIONS

The third principal source of knowledge of the NT text is the great number of quotations from the NT which are found in the writings of Christian writers of the early centuries. These quotations are so extensive that the NT could virtually be reconstructed from them without the use of NT MSS. Most of the quotations are found in Greek and Latin documents, with an appreciable amount in Syriac and some in a few other languages.

As in the case of the versions, the importance of the patristic quotations lies in the information they furnish concerning the text of the NT MSS used by the various church fathers. As in the versions, some preliminary considerations must be borne in mind in dealing with patristic quotations:

(a) Has the quotation been altered in its transmission? As in the case of the NT text itself, so also in the case of the Fathers: no autographs of their writings are extant, with all known MSS being copies removed by a longer or shorter interval from the original. This allows the possibility that the words of the quotation, as well as any other part of the MSS, may have been altered in copying. Indeed, there is more likelihood of alteration to the NT quotations than to the rest of the Father's text. This means that before NT quotations from a patristic source can properly be used, the MSS of the patristic document must themselves be submitted to textual criticism so as to determine as nearly as possible the form of the NT quotations as the Father originally quoted them.

(b) Is the quotation intended to be verbatim or is it merely a loose reference or a quotation from memory? This requires a study both of the Father's usual tendencies and of the context of the particular quotation being examined. The manner in which a NT reference is introduced may be indicative. A long quotation is more likely to have been read directly from a NT MS than quoted from memory. Even a loose allusion to a passage, on the other hand, may be textually significant by the very fact of indicating that a Father's NT text does include a questioned phrase or passage.

(c) Is it an explicit single quotation, or have parallel passages been confused or conflated (combined)? Even quotations which are seemingly intended to be verbatim sometimes show a remarkable amount of confusion between parallel passages[6]—a characteristic which may be observed in some present-day sermons and writings as well.

If these cautions are kept in mind, the patristic quotations have certain values to offer in textual criticism. The Fathers are from the early centuries, the approximate time when they wrote is known, and they may be identified more or less with particular localities. This means, then, that if the form in which a Father quoted the NT can satisfactorily be determined from the extant MSS of his works, light is thereby shed upon the form of the NT text in use in the region where and at the date when that Father lived.

The NT quotations of a number of Fathers have been studied, but much work remains to be done in order to establish the relationship of the NT text of many Fathers to the various groups and text-types of MSS.

---

[6]For example, in the Catechetical Lectures (22.1) of Cyril of Jerusalem this Father bases his argument upon what he says is St. Paul's statement: καὶ αὕτη τοῦ μακαρίου Παύλου ἡ διδασκαλία . . . αὐτὸς γὰρ ἀρτίως ἐβόα . . . ("and this is the teaching of the blessed Paul . . . for he himself precisely cries . . . "). Yet his scripture quotation does not exactly follow either 1 Cor. 11:23–25 or the parallels in the Gospels: ὅτι ἐν τῇ νυκτί, ᾗ παρεδίδοτο ὁ κύριος ἡμῶν Ἰησοῦς Χριστός, λαβὼν ἄρτον καὶ εὐχαριστήσας ἔκλασε καὶ ἔδωκε τοῖς ἑαυτοῦ μαθηταῖς λέγων· λάβετε φάγετε, τοῦτό μού ἐστι τὸ σῶμα. καὶ λαβὼν τὸ ποτήριον καὶ εὐχαριστήσας εἶπε· λάβετε, πίετε, τοῦτό μού ἐστι τὸ αἷμα (quoted by Greenlee, The Gospel Text of Cyril of Jerusalem, pp. 19–20).

Numerous Fathers are cited by various editions of the Greek
NT. The century in which the cited Fathers lived is given in
the introduction to some of the editions, including both Nestle and the Bible Societies' Greek text. In addition, Gregory's
Prolegomena to Tischendorf's Greek NT (8th major edition,
vol. 3, pp. 1129–1230) gives a comprehensive listing of Fathers,
their dates, and their writings. For detailed information concerning the life and works of the Fathers, a patrology should be
consulted.[7] The following is only a brief listing of a few of the
Fathers, with whose names the beginning student should become familiar.

Ambrose, bishop of Milan from 374 to 397, is the author of
numerous homilies, exegetical works, and moral and dogmatic
writings. His exegetical works are largely based on the OT, but
they include an exposition of Luke.

Andreas, archbishop of Caesarea in Cappadocia, about the
year 520 wrote a commentary on Revelation which also contains the complete Greek text of Revelation. This is the most
ancient extant Greek commentary on Revelation.

Athanasius, bishop of Alexandria from 328 to 373 but five
times banished by Arians and their sympathizers, is the author
of apologetic works, writings against the Arians, some exegetical
works extant in fragmentary form, and a body of festal letters.

Augustine (354–430), bishop of Hippo, is the author of a great
number of works, including philosophical, dogmatic, exegetical, and others, the most important being his *De civitate Dei.*

Basil the Great, metropolitan of Caesarea in Cappadocia from
370 to 379, is the author of a number of dogmatic, ascetic, and
other works.

John Chrysostom (ca. 344–407), patriarch of Constantinople
earned his title of "Golden-mouth" through the brilliance of his
preaching. His extant writings are the most extensive of any
Greek Father, comprised principally of homilies and commentaries on many parts of the Bible.

---

[7] E.g., Otto Bardenhewer, *Patrology;* or Berthold Altaner, *Patrology.*

Clement of Alexandria wrote an extensive introduction to Christianity during his association with the catechetical school in Alexandria, ca. 190–203.

Cyril, bishop of Alexandria from 412 to 444, is the author of apologetic and dogmatic writings, but most extensive are his exegetical works, including commentaries on numerous books of the OT and NT.

Cyril, bishop of Jerusalem ca. 350–86, is known for his catechetical lectures addressed to candidates for baptism; his lectures contain extensive biblical quotations and allusions.

Eusebius Pamphili, bishop of Caesarea in Palestine ca. 313–40, is important especially for his *Ecclesiastical History*, commentaries on several books of the Bible, and his *Evangelical Preparation* and his *Evangelical Demonstration*. In addition to other works, Eusebius assembled the Ammonian sections, into which the Gospels had previously been divided, into ten tables showing the parallel sections and thus providing a detailed Gospel harmony.

Gregory of Nazianzus (ca. 330–89), spent most of his adult life in his native Cappadocia. Most significant are his forty-five orations; a number of his letters and poems are also known.

Gregory of Nyssa, a native of Caesarea in Cappadocia, a younger brother of Basil the Great, was made bishop of Nyssa in 371 and died ca. 395. He wrote numerous exegetical works and dogmatic, ascetic, and other writings.

Irenaeus (ca. 140–210), bishop of Lyons, was born in Asia Minor and claims to have listened to Polycarp in Smyrna. His work *Against Heresies* is known in the original Greek only in quotations found in writings of other Fathers, but is extant in a very literal Latin translation made soon after the original was written.

Jerome, or Sophronius Eusebius Hieronymus (ca. 331–420), was born in Dalmatia but lived in Syria, Constantinople, Rome, and Bethlehem. He is best known for his work in producing the Latin Vulgate Bible, but he is also the author of Latin commentaries on numerous books of the Bible and various other works.

Origen (ca. 185–254) was born in Alexandria and lived most of his life there but settled in Caesarea in Palestine about 232. His Hexapla, a six–version rendering of the OT, is lost except for some Greek fragments and a Syriac translation of the Septuagint column. His exegetical writings—scholia, homilies, and commentaries—are especially important for textual studies; two works on asceticism also survive.

Primasius, bishop of Hadrumetum in Byzacena in the middle of the sixth century, is the author of a Latin commentary on Revelation which includes excerpts from earlier Latin commentators.

Tertullian (Quintus Septimius Florens Tertullianus), ca. 150–240, became a Christian ca. 195. He joined the Montanist sect ca. 202 and thereafter vehemently attacked the orthodox church. He is one of the most prolific writers of the Latin Fathers. His style is passionate and extreme. His *Apologeticum* is known in numerous and ancient MSS; many other of his writings are combined in one ninth-century MS; others are lost.

Chapter 4

❧

THE TRANSMISSION OF THE TEXT

A. HISTORY OF THE HANDWRITTEN TEXT[1]

Attention has earlier been given to the form in which the NT first appeared. It is now appropriate to study the transmission of its text down through the centuries. Only a broad outline can be presented at this point, however, with discussion of details and divergent opinions reserved for a later chapter. Some items in this history, moreover, have been anticipated in the preceding chapter, since the MSS, versions, and patristic literature were written at various times over a period of many centuries.

1. Early Period (to A.D. 325)

Although the same basic principles were at work in the transmission of the text of the NT and that of the secular classics, there were nevertheless certain factors which resulted in significant differences between the two. In the very earliest period, the NT writings were more nearly "private" writings than were the classics. This was particularly true of the epistles, but to a less extent it was true of the narrative books as well. The NT books were copied and circulated for different reasons than were the classics. Further, whereas the classics were commonly—although not always—copied by professional scribes, the NT books

---

[1] The treatment of this subject in B. H. Streeter, *The Four Gospels*, pp. 29–47, is very helpful.

were probably usually copied in this early period by Christians who were not professionally trained for the task, and no corrector (διορθωτής) was employed to check the copyist's work against his exemplar (the MS from which the copy was made). Moreover, whereas the classics were "literature" from the moment of their publication and would be copied with attention to the precise forms of the text, in the case of the NT books in the earliest period of their history the message was of paramount importance rather than such matters as word order and other details that did not affect the meaning. It appears that copyists sometimes even took the liberty to add or change minor details in the narrative books on the basis of personal knowledge, alternative tradition, or a parallel account in another book of the Bible. Christianity, an unofficial and often persecuted religion, would not have the opportunity which the classics would have of establishing an official edition of its books with which copies could be compared. Indeed, copies of the NT owned by churches, which would likely furnish the most nearly "official" text of a community, would be the very MSS most subject to confiscation and destruction in time of persecution. Finally, the expectation of Christ's imminent return was probably sufficiently prevalent among the earliest Christians that they would not be acutely concerned to preserve their books for distant centuries.

At the same time, the importance of these factors in affecting the purity of the NT text must not be exaggerated. The NT books doubtless came to be considered as "literature" soon after they began to be circulated, with attention to the precise wording required when copies were made.

The making of copies of any document of appreciable length means the introduction of errors into the text. All ancient literature demonstrates this fact. Variants are found in NT MSS of all periods. The variants which require consideration in textual criticism, however, arose for the most part in the earliest period of textual history. This period of *divergence of manuscripts* may be said to extend to the time when Christianity had established itself as the religion of the Roman Empire, although even the first half of this period likely saw the introduction of most of the variants.

This early period is likewise the period of the rise of what may be called "local texts," a factor which is interrelated with the multiplication of variants. Copies of the NT books were carried to various localities by the Christians, each MS containing its own characteristic textual variants. These MSS would then be further copied, with the resulting copies tending to contain the characteristic variants of the parent MS plus some additional errors. In this manner, over a period of time the MSS circulating in a given locality would tend to resemble each other more nearly than they would resemble the MSS of any other locality. Even within one locality, however, virtually no two MSS would be identical; and certain groups of MSS, while sharing the common "local text," would resemble each other even more closely than they would resemble other MSS of the same local text. To complicate matters, a MS of one locality might be compared with a MS of another locality and corrected by it, producing a "mixed" text.

In speaking of similarity of MSS, it must be remembered that most MSS are identical in more than three-fourths of their text. In actual practice, therefore, closely related MSS are commonly identified by "agreement in error," which includes the agreement of two or more MSS in a reading which differs from other MSS or from the common text. Agreement in a peculiar reading or in numerous small details is particularly convincing evidence of a close relationship.

The identification of the geographical region with which a given local text is associated is sometimes assisted by the text of versions and of church fathers, as indicated in the preceding chapter. Present evidence suggests that different local texts may have been current in the regions dominated by such centers as Rome, Alexandria, Caesarea or Jerusalem, and Constantinople.[2]

---

[2]See the map, "Geographical Distribution of Local Texts," in L. D. Twilley, *The Origin and Transmission of the New Testament*, p. 66.

2. The Text Standardized

When Christianity attained official status under Constantine, MSS of the NT needed no longer be kept concealed for safety. Very soon afterwards the emperor himself ordered fifty new copies of the Bible to be made for the churches of Constantinople. In this new position, there would soon arise both a greater opportunity for the official comparison of the text of various MSS and a more evident need for such comparison and for bringing together into a unified tradition the divergent streams of the local texts. Professional scribes could now be employed for copying the MSS, which would tend to reduce the amount of further variation in the text. Both of these factors combined to open what was in a sense the period of the *convergence of manuscipts*, during which the various local texts gave way to one dominant text.

With the rise of Constantinople as the center of the Greek-speaking church, it is not surprising that the local text in use there seems to have become the dominant text throughout most of the church. There was apparently some comparison of this text with other texts, resulting in something of a mixed type of text. The text seems also to have been subjected to editing, with parallel accounts tending to become harmonized, grammatical irregularities corrected, and abrupt transitions modified, producing a generally smooth text. It is not known, however, to what extent this comparison and editing of MSS was done officially and to what extent it was informal or incidental.

The evidence of the MSS indicates that the processes of standardization of the text and consequent displacement of the older text-types continued from the fourth century until the eighth, by the end of which time the standardized or "Byzantine" text had become the accepted form of the text.

Approximately 95 percent of the existing MSS of the NT are from the eighth and later centuries, and very few of these differ appreciably from the Byzantine text. This means that the witnesses for the pre-Byzantine text of the NT consist of a relatively small percentage of the MSS, mostly from the period earlier than the eighth century.

So long as MSS continued to be copied by hand there were naturally variations between them, but the text after the eighth century was almost always an essentially Byzantine text. With the invention of printing, it became possible for the first time to have a completely standardized text with an unlimited number of identical copies. The printed Greek NT was likewise basically a Byzantine type of text and continued to be so until the latter part of the nineteenth century.

B. Types of Variants

The errors and variants which are found in the MSS of the Greek NT may be classed under several headings, falling generally into two groups: those which seem to have arisen by accident, and those which seem to have been made intentionally by the scribe. More than one factor may be involved in a variant.

1. Unintentional Changes

This group comprises by far the larger number of variants in the NT MSS, including errors of a number of different types. The absence of spacing between words and the lack of punctuation and of diacritical marks in the earliest MSS help to account for many of these variants.

a. Errors of Sight. (i) Wrong division of words was easy when there were no spaces between words and no accents or breathings. In 1 Tim. 3:16 some MSS read ὁμολογοῦμεν ὡς μέγα, "we acknowledge how great," for ὁμουλογουμένως μέγα, "confessedly great"; and in Mark 10:40 some witnesses read ἄλλοις ἡτοίμασται, "it is prepared for others," instead of ἀλλ᾽ οἷς ἡτοίμασται, "but it is for those for whom it is prepared."

(ii) Confusion of one letter for another was possible both in uncial and in minuscule writing. In uncials, letters which were often similar in appearance include A Δ Λ, E Σ, O Θ, H N, and Π / IT / ΓΙ.[3] In minuscules, confusion might arise between

---

[3]Note the error of ETEN- for ΕΓΕΝ- twice in Twilley, *Origin and Transmission*, p. 42.

κ β, ει / ες / ετ, μ ν, π ω, and ζ ξ. An important variant in 1 Tim. 3:16 involves the difference between ος and θ̅ς̅—"who was manifested" or "God was manifested." Both word-division and confusion of uncial letters are seen in the variants περισ-σου εν εαυτοις / περιεσωσεν αυτους / περισσως εν εαυτοις in Mark 6:51.

(iii) *Homoioteleuton* ("similar ending") refers to an error in which the scribe's eye skips from one occurrence of a group of letters or a word to the same group of letters or word farther down the page, resulting in the omission of the intervening material in the MSS he is writing. In 1 John 2:23 many MSS thus skip from the first occurrence of τὸν πατέρα ἔχει to the second; and a similar error may have occurred in John 6:11–12, with some MSS skipping from the first τοῖς to the second. Two long omissions in Matt. 5:19–20 may be due to the occurrence of τῶν οὐρανῶν three times in these verses.

A special case of homoioteleuton involves writing a word or letter(s) once when it should be written twice; this is known as *haplography* ("single writing"). The opposite, writing a word or letter(s) twice instead of once is called *dittography*. If there is good textual support for both readings it will be a part of the problem to decide whether the error is haplography or dittography—that is, whether the original was the longer or the shorter reading. Examples of this type of variant occur in 1 Thes. 2:7, ἐγενήθημεν νήπιοι, "we became infants," and ἐγενήθημεν ἤπιοι, "we became gentle"; in Luke 7:21, ἐχαρίσατο τὸ βλέπειν in Codex Ξ instead of ἐχαρίσατο βλέπειν; and possibly ὁ θεὸς θεὸς instead of θεὸς in some MSS in Mark 12:27.

(iv) *Metathesis* ("change of place") refers to the change of order of letters or words, such as ἔλαβον for ἔβαλον in Mark 14:65, and σωτηρίαν for σωτῆρα Ἰησοῦν (C̅ P̅I̅Α̅N̅ / C̅ P̅Α̅ I̅N̅) in Acts 13:23.

(v) Various other errors of sight occur from time to time, since scribes are human and handwriting varies in form and legibility.

b. Errors of Writing. Errors which the scribe might make in writing would be similar to some of those involved in reading his exemplar, the error in this case being not in what he saw in his exemplar but in what he wrote.

c. Errors of Hearing. At a very early date various Greek vowels and diphthongs had come to be pronounced alike, a process known as *itacism*, which is likewise characteristic of modern Greek. For example, αι and ε were pronounced alike; o, ῳ, and ω were pronounced alike; ι, υ, η, ῃ, ει, οι, and υι were pronounced alike, and the rough breathing was not distinguished in pronunciation. For example, errors of hearing may at least be factors in the variants ἔχομεν / ἔχωμεν in Rom. 5:1, ἡμῶν / ὑμῶν in 1 John 1:4, and καυθήσομαι / καυχήσωμαι ("be burned"/"boast") in 1 Cor. 13:3. Confusion of ει and ι is common in the MSS, usually with no meaningful difference; but when the scribe of one MS carelessly wrote χειρῶν for χηρῶν in Luke 20:47 he changed "*widows'* houses" to "*hands'* houses"! Frequent variation between forms of the aorist subjunctive and the future indicative is likewise found in the MSS, the variation being between ω and o, and between η and ει; e.g., νικήσῃς / νικήσεις, Rom. 3:4; and ζήσομεν / ζήσωμεν, Rom. 6:2. Variations between forms of ὑμεῖς and ἡμεῖς (e.g., in 1 John 1:4), which may involve important differences in meaning, are less surprising when it is remembered that the two words were pronounced alike. In addition, other letters and sounds might sometimes be confused. Codex D, by erroneously writing μή instead of με in Mark 14:31, makes Peter timidly assert that he will never deny Jesus "if it is *not* necessary to die"!

d. Errors of Memory. The scribe might forget a precise word while remembering the meaning, and thus substitute a synonym (e.g., ὀφθαλμῶν for ὀμμάτων in Matt. 20:34); he might make a change of word order (e.g., καλοὺς ποιεῖ / ποιεῖ καλούς in Matt. 7:17 and πονηρίᾳ πλεονεξίᾳ κακίᾳ / πονηρίᾳ κακίᾳ πλεονεξίᾳ / κακίᾳ πονηρίᾳ πλεονεξίᾳ in Rom. 1:29); or he might unconsciously be influenced by a parallel passage (e.g., the addition of αὐτοῦ ἀκούσεσθε, "you shall hear him," from

Deut. 18:15 in Acts 7:37, and the addition of διὰ τοῦ αἵματος αὐτοῦ, "through his blood," in Col. 1:14 from Eph. 1:7), although variants based on parallel passages are probably more frequently intentional variations.

   e. Errors of Judgment. Remembering that a copyist might not be thinking carefully of the meaning of what he was writing, it may be seen how he might misunderstand or overlook an abbreviation (e.g., ος / $\overline{\theta\varsigma}$ in 1 Tim. 3:16); or might include in his text what had been intended as a marginal note of explanation (which may account for the origin of the reference to the angel troubling the water in John 5:3–4); or might fail to include something which had been omitted in the text and added later in the margin.

   The scribe might also mistakenly copy a more familiar word for a less common word which looked or sounded similar, even if the meaning was quite different; Codex Ξ thus reads in Luke 6:42, ". . . the *fruit* (καρπός) which is in your eye" instead of "the *speck* (κάρφος)."[4]

2. Intentional Changes

   Although much less numerous than the unintentional changes, intentional changes comprise a significant number of errors. They derive for the most part from attempts by scribes to improve the text in various ways. There is virtually no evi-

---

   [4]Many similar errors can be found in contemporary English, and it is instructive to take notice of them. In my own experience, printers have made devastating omissions by homoioteleuton; a typist has written, "is *not* being prepared by a committee of scholars" for "is *now* being prepared," and "ultra-violent" for "ultra-violet"; I myself typed "Newberry Librarry Library" for "Newberry Library" in a letter and only later discovered the error; a high class advertisement of the book, *Christmas Is Always*, shows a simulated picture of the book-jacket with the title given as *Christmas As Always*. People sing "Crowns and *thorns* may perish" in a familiar gospel song, apparently subconsciously thinking of Jesus' crown of thorns; and preachers mistakenly refer to "judgment to come" instead of "judgment" in John 16:8, under the influence of Acts 24:25.

dence that heretical or destructive variants have been deliberately introduced into the MSS.

a. Grammatical and Linguistic Changes. These include "correction" of the first aorist endings on second aorist verbs (as ἦλθαν / ἦλθον in Mark 6:29), assimilation of non-assimilated forms (as λήψομαι for λήμψομαι in Matt. 10:41), and ἐγκαίνια for ἐνκαίνια in John 10:22), and various other alterations of what appeared to the scribe to be an incorrect or less desirable form (e.g., ἀλλ᾽ / ἀλλά in Rom. 1:21, ἑαυτοῖς / αὐτοῖς in Rom. 1:24, and τὸν Ἰησοῦν / Ἰησοῦν in Rom. 8:11).

This type of change might result from a scribe's understanding a different syntax than that implied by his exemplar: e.g., in Rom. 3:29 μόνον / μόνος / μόνων each give an understandable but different sense; in Rom. 4:8 οὗ gives the meaning "whose sin . . . ," while ᾧ implies "to whom (the Lord will not account) sin"; and in Rom. 4:11 περιτομῆς gives the sense "he received the sign of circumcision," while περιτομήν yields the meaning "he received circumcision as a sign."

b. Liturgical Changes. If a NT passage were used in a slightly altered form, this change might find its way into some MSS. The doxology to the Lord's Prayer in Matt. 6:13 may have had this origin; and the changes made in the opening words of lectionary passages sometimes doubtless became variants in the MSS.

c. Elimination of Apparent Discrepancies. These variants may include discrepancies of biblical reference, as the change from "Isaiah the prophet" to "the prophets" in Mark 1:2. They may involve historical difficulties, as "on the third day" for "after three days" in Mark 10:34. They may be attempts to harmonize parallels: thus the Lord's Prayer in Luke 11:2–4 is "filled out" from Matt. 6:9–13; δικαιοσύνην in Matt. 6:1 is mistakenly changed to ἐλεημοσύνην to agree with 6:2; and in Luke 15:21 several good MSS make the Prodigal Son complete the speech that in 15:19 he said he would make to his father. Other variants may attempt to correct an error of fact: in 1 Pet. 2:23 a scribe, apparently thinking of how Jesus gave himself up to Pilate instead of how he committed his soul to God, changed δικαίως ("righteously") to ἀδίκως ("unrighteously"); and in Rom. 4:19 the addition or omission of οὐ ("he considered" or "he did not consider") may reflect attempts to correct what seemed to be a misstatement concerning Abraham's thoughts.

d. Harmonization. Hamonization of parallel passages may be an intentional change. This type of variant is frequently encountered in the Synoptic Gospels (cf. Matt. 19:17 with Mark 10:18; the variation on words for "needle's eye" in Matt. 19:24, Mark 10:25, and Luke 18:25; and numerous other "parallel" variants noted in the critical apparatus of various editions of the NT).

e. Conflation. Conflation is the combining of two or more variants into one reading: e.g., in Luke 24:53 the variants εὐλογοῦντες and αἰνοῦντες are apparently conflated to form a third reading, αἰνοῦντες καὶ εὐλογοῦντες; in Rom. 3:23 εἰς πάντας καὶ ἐπὶ πάντας may be a conflation of the two other variants, εἰς πάντας and ἐπὶ πάντας; and the longer reading in the passage concerning "salting" in Mark 9:49 is probably a conflation.

f. Attempts to Correct a MS Error. The scribe may have attempted to correct what he thought was an error in his exemplar. Thus in Rom. 8:2 σε may be the original which was changed to με by a well-meaning scribe because of the sense of the previous verses; and in Rev. 1:5 a scribe may have thought he was restoring the original text by changing λύσαντι, "loosed (us from our sins)," to λούσαντι, "washed."

g. Doctrinal Changes. Intentional doctrinal changes which have received any appreciable MSS support have almost invariably been changes in the direction of orthodoxy or stronger doctrinal emphasis. Movement toward a doctrinally weaker text is more likely to be an unintentional change. Variants that seem intended to strengthen a doctrinal statement or introduce an accepted doctrine include the Trinitarian passage of 1 John 5:7–8, which has no non-suspect support in the Greek

MSS; the addition of "and fasting" to "prayer" in Mark 9:29; the additions at the end of Rom. 8:1 and 1 Cor. 6:20; and the passage concerning the resurrection in 1 Cor. 15:51. No Christian doctrine, however, hangs upon a debatable text; and the student of the NT must beware of wanting the text to be more orthodox or doctrinally stronger than is the inspired original.[5]

---

[5]Instances of intentional textual variation can likewise be cited in contemporary English, including such diverse examples as the alteration of recent editions of some children's fairy stories to soften or remove references to violence or death; the change of the line "And down he run" to "The mouse ran down," in the well-known Mother Goose rhyme, sacrificing the rhyme in the interests of good grammar; the alteration of "For such a worm as I" to "For sinners such as I" in one gospel song and "Offspring of a virgin's womb" to "Here to make his humble home" in another, both to make a less objectionable text; and the substitution of "Prone to love thee, Lord, I feel it; Prone to serve the God I love" for "Prone to wander, Lord, I feel it; Prone to leave the God I love" in the hymn, "Come Thou Fount," in the interest of a particular doctrine.

Chapter 5

❧

THE TEXT IN PRINT

A. THE ESTABLISHMENT OF THE "RECEIVED TEXT" (1516–1633)

In the middle of the fifteenth century the world of literature was revolutionized by the invention of printing from movable type. For the first time it became possible to reproduce a document in an unlimited number of copies, and to have these copies absolutely identical in their text. The difference this invention made for the civilized world is almost beyond comprehension.

The age of manuscripts was virtually at an end. This does not mean that every scribe laid down his pen as the first printed sheet came from the press; some manuscripts continued to be copied for generations. Yet the printing press signaled the beginning of a new age in which literature would no longer depend upon single copies tediously made by hand, and when books could be owned by the masses instead of the wealthy few alone.

The first document to come from the printing press was a printed single-sheet indulgence to be sold by the church in 1454, from the press of Fust and Gutenberg in Mainz, Germany. Two years later, in 1456, the first Bible was published: a Latin Vulgate, a beautiful work of folio size, of which some forty copies are still in existence. This edition is known as the *Gutenberg Bible* (sometimes as the Mazarin Bible because the copy which first attracted the attention of scholars was in the library of Cardinal Mazarin in Paris).

In the fifteenth century biblical scholars were comparatively little concerned about the Greek text of the NT; the Latin Vulgate was their Bible. It was therefore more than half a century after printing had begun that a complete Greek NT came from the press. In 1502 Cardinal Ximenes of Toledo, Spain, began the preparation of an edition of the Greek Bible. The OT was to have the Hebrew, Latin, and Greek texts in parallel columns (with the Latin in the center, the cardinal's editors stated, just as Jesus hung on the cross between two thieves), and the NT was to be in Latin and Greek. The NT volume was printed in 1514, but was withheld from publication until the OT volumes were printed. These were completed in 1517, but the approval of the pope was not given until 1520, and the work was apparently not actually available until 1522. This Bible came to be known as the *Complutensian Polyglot*; "polyglot" ("many tongues") because of the three languages used, and "Complutensian" from Complutum, the Latin name for Alcalá, the city in which it was produced.

Although the Complutensian was the first edition of the NT to be *printed*, it was not the first to be *published*—actually placed on the market. A Swiss printer, Froben, hearing of the Cardinal's anticipated edition, sought out the scholar *Erasmus* in April 1515 and asked him to prepare an edition of the Greek NT as quickly as possible. Erasmus had been anxious to undertake such a task and set about it willingly, using no more than six MSS which happened to be available. His only non-Byzantine MS of any antiquity was Codex 1, and he does not seem to have leaned very heavily upon its text. Erasmus began the preparation of his edition in September 1515, and it was published only seven months later, in March 1516.[1] His one MS of Revelation was mutilated, and he supplied the missing portions,

---

[1] See the photographs of Erasmus' first edition and of the Complutensian Polyglot in Kenyon, *Our Bible and the Ancient Manuscripts*, Plates 10–11, facing pp. 102 and 103.

including all of the last six verses of the book, by retranslating from the Latin. Erasmus published four subsequent editions but consulted few additional MSS and made only minor changes and corrections in his text.

The third edition of Erasmus was the first to contain the famous "heavenly witnesses" passage of 1 John 5:7–8. This passage was contained in the Vulgate, and when Stunica, one of Ximenes' editors, protested its omission from the Greek text Erasmus rashly promised to include it in a later edition if it could be found in a single Greek MS. It was accordingly produced, from a MS (Codex 61) very possibly prepared for the purpose, and Erasmus dutifully fulfilled his promise in his edition of 1522. He again omitted it in his later editions; but it was the third edition which primarily influenced textual tradition, and the "heavenly witnesses" thus found their place in the Greek text.

Robert Estienne, frequently known as *Stephanus,* the form in which he Latinized his name, was one of a family of printers at Paris and later at Geneva. He published four editions of the Greek NT between 1546 and 1551, using the text of Erasmus and the Complutensian with some consultation of about fifteen MSS. His third edition, which he called the Regia, was a large folio-sized volume published in 1550. This edition was the first Greek NT with something like a critical apparatus, giving variant readings from the fifteen MSS he had consulted and from the Complutensian in the margin. It was this text which became the standard text in Great Britain and the United States. Estienne's fourth edition (1551) contained the same Greek text as the third edition, but it is notable for the first introduction of the verse numeration which is still in use. Our chapter divisions had been introduced about the year 1205 by Stephen Langton, archbishop of Canterbury.

Theodore Beza, the French Protestant scholar, published nine editions of the Greek NT from 1565 to 1604. Their text was essentially that of Erasmus and Stephanus, but Beza's reputation helped to promote and to set the form of the printed Greek text.

Bonaventure and Abraham Elzevir, publishers in Holland, published seven editions of the Greek NT between 1624 and 1678. Their purpose was commercial rather than critical; their text was based on those of Stephanus and of Beza. Their editions were widely sold, and their second edition (1633) became the standard text in continental Europe. In the preface to their second edition they included the optimistic statement: "Textum ergo habes, nunc ab omnibus receptum: in quo nihil immutatum aut corruptum damus" ("You have therefore the text now received by all: in which we give nothing altered or corrupt"). From this statement there came into use the term "Textus Receptus" ("Received Text"), which is still applied to the Stephanus third edition of 1550 and the Elzevir second edition of 1633.

Thus the standardized but inferior text which supplanted the ancient local texts, and whose general form became the manuscript text for eight centuries, became likewise the accepted form of the printed text—its precise printed form being the result of mere chance. While it is a generally Byzantine text, therefore, it is not a precise Byzantine text and sometimes does not represent the text of the minuscule MSS and the late text. Sometimes its text is better than the Byzantine; at other times it has relatively little support of any kind—e.g., Matt. 18:6 επι, Matt. 27:46 λαμα (spelling), Mark 10:24 επι τοις, and Acts 5:41 ονοματος αυτου. How inferior it is in Revelation, where it is the worst, may easily be seen in Tischendorf's apparatus, where he shows the Textus Receptus sometimes with little or no support of any kind—e.g., 13:16 δωση, 14:8 αλλος αγγελος, 15:3 των αγιων, and 20:5 οι δε . . . . ανεζησαν . . . . εως. . . .

The TR is not a "bad" or misleading text, either theologically or practically. Technically, however, it is far from the original text. Yet three centuries were to pass before scholars won the struggle to replace this hastily assembled text with a text which gave evidence of being closer to the NT autographs.

B. THE ACCUMULATION OF TEXTUAL EVIDENCE (1633–1830)

By 1633, so great had become the interest in the Greek NT and the demand for it that a hundred different editions had been published, virtually all of them substantially the text of Erasmus and Stephanus. The NT was now generally available to churches and individuals. The time had come when scholars could turn their attention to examining the text to see whether it could be improved. With this scholarly interest in the text, old MSS began more and more to come to light and attention began to be given to MSS which were already known. Study of the MSS naturally revealed many differences between their texts and that of the printed texts. Scholars began to compare the variant readings, forming judgments of the relative value of variants and of MSS. In this way a great deal of material was accumulated which both furnished materials for later scholars to use and stimulated interest in further discoveries and study of the MSS. While for two centuries after the Elzevir editions the printed text continued to be close to that of Erasmus and Stephanus, the period was characterized by the accumulation of readings of the MSS and the evaluation of the evidence, which were to lead to a demand for a printed text better than the Textus Receptus.

John Mill, building upon foundations laid by the previous work of several other scholars, published a large edition of the Greek NT in 1707. His text was that of the third edition of Stephanus with only a few changes, and with a critical apparatus of the readings of seventy-eight MSS, several versions, and some patristic writers. Probably no one contributed more information from these sources of the text for the next century than did Mill. It would have been impossible for him to print a text differing substantially from the TR and have it accepted; he was violently attacked even for the changes which he did make and for his notes which showed his preference for numerous readings that differed from the TR.

Richard Bentley issued no NT text but was an influential scholar. He defended the study of textual criticism and the importance of studying the MSS against those who attacked Mill's work. Bentley proposed the printing of a revised Greek and Vulgate text, which was likewise opposed by those who considered the Textus Receptus sacrosanct; but the project was far vaster than Bentley apparently realized and was not carried out.

Johannes Albrecht Bengel published a text in 1734 in which he deserted the TR only when a reading he preferred had already appeared elsewhere in print, but he indicated other preferred readings in the margin. The importance of Bengel's work is that he is the first to attempt to group and classify the witnesses to the text, calling them African and Asiatic. He is thus in a sense the father of modern textual criticism.

Johann Jakob Wettstein in 1751–52 published the received text in two volumes, indicating what he thought were the true readings in his critical apparatus. His unique contribution is that he was the first to use the system of citing uncial MSS by capital letters and minuscules by arabic numbers. His textual theory, on the other hand, defended the witness of the late MSS, maintaining that the oldest MSS had been contaminated by the Latin.

Johann Salomo Semler did not publish a text, but he built on Bengel's classification of witnesses into Alexandrian, Western, and Eastern families.

Semler's theory was popularized and extended by his pupil, *Johann Jakob Griesbach*, one of the most important of textual scholars, who published three editions of the NT between 1774 and 1806 and also collated a large number of MSS. Griesbach proposed three families of witnesses in the Gospels: (1) Alexandrian, including MSS C K L 1 13 33 69, the Bohairic and some other versions, and the quotations of Origen, Eusebius, and some other Fathers; (2) Western, including Codex D and the Latin versions and Fathers; and (3) Byzantine, including A and the later uncials and most minuscules, which he considered inferior to the other two families. In the Pauline epistles he recognized two families, Alexandrian and Western. In addition to his critical apparatus, Griesbach gave a list of readings with symbols indicating, in his opinion, the degree of probability that they were original readings.

During this period, in addition to collations of MSS and the citation of their readings in editions of the Greek NT, the full text of several important MSS, including Codex A and Codex D, were published in 1800. The work of *Johannes Martin Augustinus Scholz*, which extends into the following period, may appropriately be mentioned here. He traveled extensively through Europe and assembled a catalogue of MSS, including in it lists already published and adding to it the identification of other MSS located in many libraries, thus showing scholars where much valuable future work lay.

C. THE STRUGGLE FOR A CRITICAL TEXT (1830–82)

The exact form of the early printed texts came largely by chance, depending upon the particular MSS which were available to Erasmus and others of the earliest editors. Yet most of the MSS which an editor was likely to have at hand were generally Byzantine in character. By the early part of the nineteenth century, however, scores of Greek MSS from earlier centuries, and something of the texts of versions and of patristic quotations, were known. Scholars were coming to see, moreover, that many readings which differed from the TR, especially readings from the older MSS, were clearly preferable to the TR. It was no easy matter, however, to print a text which differed substantially from the TR. Voices were raised even in the highest circles against disturbing what was considered to be the sacred original text—considered to be so simply because it was the form of the text which had long been accepted. At the same time, the increasing evidence could not forever be disregarded.

Some attempts had previously been made to change the printed text, but these had for the most part been a relatively few changes in what was still basically the TR. The first editor to abandon the TR was Dr. Edward Wells, with his edition of 1709–19.

His edition was largely ignored at the time, however.[2] The credit for abandoning the TR is therefore generally given to Karl Lachmann. Lachmann was a classicist and not a theologian; consequently, he was unaware of how violent the criticism against his work might be. He set the TR aside completely and constructed a text from what he believed were the most ancient witnesses. His first edition was published in 1831 with no explanation of how he had arrived at his text, but merely a statement that a certain theological journal contained an article in which he had set forth his principles. He could hardly have better succeeded in inciting criticism against his text. In 1842–50 he published a second edition, this time with a full statement of his principles, which silenced some criticism and won support for his text. Lachmann's great contribution, therefore, is that his was the first generally recognized "critical text"—i.e., a text constructed according to principles of textual criticism. His weakness was that he ignored groupings of MSS and thus regressed from the advances which had been made in this area.

Samuel Prideaux Tregelles exercised an influence in England, as did Lachmann on the Continent, toward the rejection of the TR in favor of a critical text. His edition of the NT, embodying his own critical text, was published in 1857–79. His critical principles were fairly sound, and his apparatus presented the textual evidence in convenient form. Tregelles likewise did much valuable work in collating and describing NT MSS.

Perhaps the greatest name in NT textual criticism is that of *Constantin von Tischendorf.* This German scholar seems to have dedicated his life to discovering and editing as many NT MSS as possible and to publishing editions of the Greek NT. He made numerous tours of Europe and the Middle East in his quests. He read and published in Paris the text of the important palimpsest Codex C. He discovered and brought to light one of the most famous of all MSS, Codex Sinaiticus (א), in the Monas-

---

[2] Metzger, *The Text of the New Testament,* 3d ed., p. 109.

tery of St. Catherine on Mt. Sinai. Altogether he published the texts of twenty-one uncial MSS of various length and collated or copied the texts of more than twenty others.

Tischendorf was equally industrious in editing the Greek NT, publishing eight editions between 1841 and 1872. His "eighth major edition" (1869–72) contains a critical apparatus which has never been equaled in comprehensiveness of citation of Greek MSS, versions, and patristic evidence. A century later it is still indispensable for serious work in the text of the NT. Tischendorf's influence was likewise, of course, in support of the principle of a critical text, although his own text in his eighth edition leans too heavily on the text of Codex ℵ. A volume of prolegomena, comprising volume three of the eighth major edition, was edited by *Caspar René Gregory* after the death of Tischendorf and published in 1894. This volume contains an enormous amount of information concerning the witnesses of the NT text.

The climax to this third period of the printed text comes in the joint labor of two Cambridge University scholars who rank with Tischendorf for fame in the field of textual criticism, *Brooke Foss Westcott* (later bishop of Durham) and *Fenton John Anthony Hort*, professor of divinity. For twenty-eight years they worked together on a critical edition of the Greek NT together with a volume setting forth with meticulous care their textual principles. These two volumes were published in 1881–82 under the title, *The New Testament in the Original Greek*. They had previously made their text available to the committee producing the 1881 English Revised NT, and their work is reflected in this version. Westcott and Hort's views were not completely new, of course; they built on the foundations laid by Lachmann, Tregelles, Griesbach, and Tischendorf, who helped pave the way for the acceptance of a critial text. Other factors favorable to the text of WH include the use of their text in the Revised Version of the NT, the thoroughness with which they explained their views in their volume of introduction, and the fact that their text was printed in a handy, easily usuable volume without the added bulk of an extensive critical apparatus. All things considered, the influence of WH upon all subsequent work in the history of the text has never been equaled. Their edition of the NT is likewise still considered one of the standard editions of the Greek text.

With the work of Westcott and Hort the TR was at last vanquished. In the future, whatever form an editor's text might take, he or she would be free to construct it with reference to the principles of textual criticism without being under the domination of the Textus Receptus.

❖

Chapter 6

THE AGE OF THE CRITICAL TEXT

A. THE TEXTUAL THEORY OF WESTCOTT AND HORT[1]

The textual theory of WH underlies virtually all subsequent work in NT textual criticism. Although both the work of recent scholars and the texts of MSS discovered since WH have brought about modifications of their principles, their work is so fundamental that it is appropriate to give a summary of their theory.

When faced with a variant reading in the text, the instinctive reaction is to accept the reading which seems most naturally to fit the context. At the same time, it is recognized that many errors in the MSS are likely due to the fact that a scribe misunderstood the text and changed it to a reading which seemed easier to understand or more natural. Therefore, the reading which is at first glance harder to understand in the context often proves to be original. Similarly, the reading from which the other readings could most likely have developed is to be preferred as the original. Further, intentional changes were more likely to be additions, as explanations or from other traditions, rather than omissions; thus a shorter reading is generally preferable.

Since these principles of "intrinsic probability" may be subject to differences of interpretation by different individuals, it is

---

[1] Material in this section is drawn largely from Kenyon, *Handbook*, pp. 295–306. See also Metzger, *Text*, pp. 129–35, 156ff.

desirable to strengthen the basis for decision by applying these principles to a large number of passages in a given MS so as to determine the extent to which the MS generally has readings which are preferred. A MS with preferred readings in instances in which the principles of criticism yield a fairly certain conclusion will then tend to be trusted in instances in which the intrinsic probability is uncertain. In other words, an adequate knowledge of the MSS involved, as well as of textual principles, is necessary.

Still more assurance may be gained if the various MSS and witnesses are grouped together into families having a closely related text. In this way the errors of an individual MS are eliminated and a reading will be that of the family—and thus of the family's common ancestor, which will be more ancient than any member of the family. The individual MSS of the family may also in this manner be evaluated for their degree of fidelity to the text of the family.

It will now be possible to return to the variants one by one and to confirm or modify the first judgment, in which only intrinsic probability was considered, by the additional knowledge of the general textual character of the witnesses and of the families.

The steps of the procedure, then, are as follows: (1) study individual readings on the basis of intrinsic probability; (2) evaluate the individual witnesses; (3) determine the family groupings of the witnesses; and (4) return to the individual readings to confirm or revise conclusions.

The conclusions from intrinsic probability are called "internal evidence." The testimony of MSS, versions, etc. is known as "external evidence."

When the MSS and other witnesses are examined for family groupings, they tend to fall into four groups:

(1) Most of the minuscule MSS, the later uncials, and many of the later versions and Fathers, but with no witness earlier than Chrysostom (4th cent.). Westcott-Hort designated this the "Syrian" text, believing that it originated in Syria. (This text-type must not be confused with the Syriac version.)

(2) A much smaller group of witnesses, including ℵ B L T 33, the Bohairic version, and a few other witnesses. This is termed by WH the "Neutral" text.

(3) A group which is less distinct than the others, largely composed of members of the "Neutral" group when they differ from the reading of Codex B. Westcott-Hort called this the "Alexandrian" text.

(4) A small group whose best-known Greek MSS are D and D_2 (05 and 06), together with a few minuscules, the Old Latin version, and almost all the Fathers of the second and third centuries. This is known as the "Western" text.

The general view of WH concerning the early history of the text is somewhat as follows:

Variants came into the NT at a very early stage, at which time scribes felt free to make minor changes in the text, especially the Gospels, in accordance with other traditions in circulation or to agree with a parallel account, or to substitute synonyms, paraphrase a sentence, and to make other variations. Thus by the end of the second century the "Western" text had arisen, characterized by extensive variation from the original text. Although this text is quite early in origin, the principles of intrinsic probability weigh against it in general. It is generally longer than the preferred text. In a number of notable instances, however, it has a shorter reading in which the Western text alone may have preserved the original, while all others have incorporated additions or "interpolations" (hence these readings are, according to WH, "Western non-interpolations"). Even so, a reading with only Western support cannot be accepted without some reservation.

In another area a different influence was being brought to bear upon the text. Alexandria was the home of criticism of the Greek classics. Hence the NT MSS were looked upon with literary eyes; the unsophisticated style of spoken Greek and the unclassical literary and grammatical Greek forms of the NT authors were altered by stylistic changes which were relatively minor in comparison with the Western text and did not disturb the essential accuracy of the text. Thus the "Alexandrian" text is characterized.

After Christianity attained official status in the fourth century, attempts began to be made, officially or unofficially, to deal with the divergencies in the text, aiming at combining readings where appropriate, removing obscurities, harmonizing parallels, and in general to produce a smooth text free from difficulties. Thus arose the "Syrian" text, which was smooth and sensible, yet lacking in the vigor and occasional ruggedness of the original.

One numerically small group of witnesses seems to have escaped the corruptions of all three other text-types and to have preserved the text virtually in its original form. This is the "Neutral" text. It is represented especially in the agreement of B and א, together with a few other witnesses. Sometimes the secondary witnesses desert the Neutral text to follow an Alexandrian variant, leaving the original text in B and א with little additional support. The text of B, moreover, is so superior that its text must always be given close attention, and in frequent instances the text of B is decisive over all other witnesses.

The text of WH is therefore essentially a "Neutral" or "B א" text or even a "B" text. For example, in Rom. 2:16 WH read ᾗ ἡμέρᾳ with the sole support of B against all other witnesses, and in Rom. 4:1 they read Ἀβραὰμ τὸν προπάτορα ἡμῶν supported by B, three minuscules, and two Fathers. They sometimes place in brackets, indicating doubt of their genuineness, words or phrases omitted by B when virtually all other witnesses include the words, as in the instance of the third ἐν in Mark 4:20 and αὐτοῖς in Mark 9:31. At the same time, their devotion to B is not absolute; e.g., they omit υἱοῦ θεοῦ in Mark 1:1 against B D; in Rom. 3:11 they desort B to read ἐκζητῶν supported by G C and two Fathers; and in Rom. 7:25 they read χάρις δὲ τῷ θεῷ with limited support which includes neither B nor א.

B. Defense of the Textus Receptus

The work of WH brought about the final dethronement of the TR and the establishment of the principle of a critical text.

This period likewise saw a substantial scholarly defense of the Textus Receptus. This defense rested largely in the hands of F. H. A. Scrivener and especially J. W. Burgon and Edward Miller. The latter two men exerted their joint influence in exceedingly strenuous opposition to WH.

The arguments of Burgon and Miller were primarily three-fold. In the first place, they insisted that the acceptance of the traditional text by the church for fifteen hundred years was proof of its integrity, since God would not have permitted the church to follow a corrupt text. This argument, however, breaks on the fact that the traditional text is not a "bad" or heretical text; it presents the same Christian message as the critical text. More-over, until the invention of printing the church had never fol-lowed a rigidly uniform text; many variants were always present within the MSS used by the church down through the centuries.

In the second place, Burgon and Miller argued, it was incred-ible that the testimony of hundreds of later MSS and witnesses should be set aside in favor of a very few supposedly early wit-nesses. The answer to this argument was that this was precisely what scholars had long accepted in the case of secular litera-ture. In the ancient classics which were extant in numerous MSS, in every case scholars depended upon a very few MSS for an authoritative text.

The third argument was that the traditional text was actually older and intrinsically superior. The fallacy in this argument was that the antiquity of a "Syrian" (i.e., Byzantine) reading could be shown only when the Byzantine text was supported by one of the pre-Byzantine texts, which proved nothing in favor of the Byzantine, since WH maintained that Syrian readings were largely derived from the pre-Syrian texts. That the traditional text was intrinsically superior was more nearly a matter of sub-jective opinion; but extensive comparison of text-types has left most scholars convinced that the late text is in general inferior, not superior.

With the death of Burgon and Miller serious scholarly sup-port of the TR virtually ceased for many years. Then in 1956

Edward F. Hills, who had done work in NT textual criticism at Harvard and received the Th.D. degree from that institution, published a book, *The King James Version Defended* (Des Moines, Iowa: Christian Research Press, 1956), in which he argued for the authenticity not only of the late text but even for the specific form of that text underlying the King James Version, including the Trinity passage of 1 John 5:7–8.

Hills's book evidently gained little scholarly notice. However, more recently the defense of the Byzantine text has found some new defenders. Recognizing that the TR at times was not supported by even the Byzantine text, editors modified the TR at those points, resulting in what was now called the Majority Text, since it was the text supported by a majority of the ancient manuscripts. Wilbur N. Pickering, a Wycliffe Bible translator, defended this form of the text in his Ph.D. program at the University of Toronto; his study was published as *The Identity of the New Testament Text.* Two scholars then at Dallas Theological Seminary, Zane C. Hodges and Arthur L. Farstad, have published their reconstructions of this text under the title, *The Greek New Testament According to the Majority Text.*

Without pressing the argument further, let it simply be said that the Majority Text, like its near relatives the Byzantine text and the TR, characteristically fails the test of the basic principle of textual criticism: viz., that the reading from which the other reading or readings most likely arose is generally original.

C. The Work of von Soden[2]

Shortly before the turn of the century a wealthy German woman provided generous financial assistance to Hermann Freiherr von Soden to produce a text of the NT on a scale never before equaled. Von Soden, an American-born professor in

---

[2]See Kenyon, *Handbook*, 52–55, 363–69, and Lake, 77–84, 89–90, for somewhat more detailed discussions, and the helpful summary in Metzger, *Text*, pp. 139–43.

Berlin, was to hire trained assistants to examine all known MSS of the NT both in Greek and in the ancient versions. From this tremendous undertaking there came a printed text of the NT with a large critical apparatus and an exceedingly lengthy volume of descriptions of MSS and of von Soden's textual theory.

While von Soden made some valuable contributions to textual studies, and an acquaintance with his work is essential for the serious textual student, his work in its primary objectives was perhaps the greatest disappointment in modern textual criticism. Its shortcomings were heightened both by the great amount of time and money which had been expended in the project and also by the years of anticipation during which scholars could learn nothing of von Soden's theories prior to the publication of his work.

Von Soden's textual theory was radically different from that of WH. He identified three principal texts in the extant witnesses, which he designated by Greek letters:

(1) The *K* text (Κοινή or "common" text), so called because it includes the mass of the late witnesses. It is approximately equivalent to the Syrian text of WH. The *K* text is in turn subdivided into numerous families representing various stages in its presumed development and various influences exerted upon it.

(2) The *H* text, so called because von Soden believed the scholar Hesychius (Ἡσύχιος) had produced it. The *H* text includes the Neutral and Alexandrian texts of WH.

(3) The *I* or Jerusalem (Ἰερουσαλήμ) text includes the Western text of WH together with much additional material. The *I* text is subdivided into several families.

Von Soden believed that of these three texts, the *K* text was worst and the *I* text was best, although the *H* text was generally corrupted from the original only in matters of style. He proposed to reach the archetype or common ancestor of these three texts (1) by rejecting readings harmonized to a parallel passage; (2) where the preceding rule is insufficient, by rejecting the reading in the Gospels which has been accommodated to Matthew (since Matthew was the most popular Gospel and would tend to influence the form of parallels in other Gospels); and (3) in other instances by accepting the agreement of two out of the three texts. The archetype thus arrived at von Soden labelled "*I-H-K.*"

The determination of *I-H-K*, according to von Soden, gives approximatley a fourth-century text. *I-H-K* differs appreciably from the original text, however, due to the fact that Tatian's Diatessaron, originally written in Greek, has exercised a widespread influence, not only in producing harmonization in the Gospels but also in various ways throughout the NT. By eliminating the corrupting influence of Tatian, the less extensive influence of Marcion in the epistles, and other influences, von Soden believed that he could reach the NT text of ca. A.D. 140 and that the original text had been altered but little prior to this date.

Von Soden's *H* text is generally acceptable. His *K* text is likewise generally acceptable, and his classification of subgroups of the *K* text is helpful in the study of the development of the late text. His *I* text, however, is much too inclusive and is most helpful only when his subgroups of this text are dealt with individually. One of the most dubious features of von Soden's theory, however, is the influence which he attributes to Tatian. Although a century after von Soden's work scholars still have only the slightest direct knowledge of Tatian's labors and are almost entirely dependent upon indirect information such as the Gospel harmonies of much later versions, and although nothing is known of any work by Tatian beyond the Gospels, von Soden not only claimed to be able to detect the influence of Tatian throughout the NT but even made this factor a cornerstone of his theory. His relative neglect of the versions, moreover, is a further weakness.

It would be to von Soden's credit if it could be demonstrated that he had in fact established the fourth-century text in his *I-H-K*, and especially so if he could be shown to have discovered the text of the mid-second century. The latter, however, is especially doubtful. Even so, he is surely mistaken in assuming that the text of A.D. 140 would be essentially the original NT text.

It is much more probable that most of the variations of concern to textual critics had already arisen before the middle of the second century.

A further factor weighing somewhat against the work of von Soden was the discovery, as time went by, that his collations of MSS were not always reliable or complete. This factor raised some additional questions concerning his theory, but it is of more practical concern in the use of his collations in the critical apparatus of his NT text. A further criticism of his apparatus is the fact that his presentation of the evidence is so complicated that it requires the most careful concentration to avoid misunderstanding and mistakes in reading it; and even when this pitfall is avoided, his method of presenting the evidence is such that it is often simply impossible to understand what some of the MSS actually read. His apparatus, moreover, is tendentious—i.e., he seems to try to draw conclusions for the reader instead of merely presenting the evidence as objectively as possible.[3]

The element of von Soden's presentation which will probably strike the beginning student with dismay, however, is his system of numeration of the MSS, which may be summarized as follows: MSS of the Gospels are preceded by the letter ε (i.e., εὐαγγέλιον), MSS of Acts or the epistles by letter α (i.e., ἀπόστολος), and MSS which include both sections by the letter δ (i.e., διαθήκη), all either with or without Revelation. In actual citation of evidence the ε or α is generally omitted in the apparatus but the δ must always be written. Thus in Acts "3" would indicate α3; in the Gospels 3 would be ε3; but δ3 would always be written δ3. Certain other prefixed letters are also used for special groups of MSS. The prefixed letter is followed by a number designed to

---

[3] For example, the apparatus may state that a given reading "a" is supported by the K text and by Tatian (which for von Soden immediately condemns it), and that reading "b" is supported by the H text "except . . . " and by the I text "except. . . . " Yet the "exceptions" belatedly admit that reading "a" is not a pure K reading, but that it has support from H and I witnesses as well.

indicate both a further identification of the contents of the MS and its date.[4] While such an informational system of numeration might seem to be desirable, the means by which von Soden's system gives this information is bewilderingly complicated. In addition, the adoption of von Soden's system would require a complete abandonment of the previously used designations. A limitation to any such informational system of numeration, moreover, is the fact that dates of MSS are not always certain, and conclusions are subject to alteration. Even more surprisingly, von Soden's system lumps together all MSS earlier than the tenth century, the period in which discrimination of date is most important; he indicates dates by centuries only for MSS of the tenth century and later, the period in which the exact century is much less important. For the beginning student, therefore, the best procedure is to use Kraft's "key" to von Soden's numeration[5] without attempting to remember the implications of von Soden's numbers.

One of the most significant contributions of von Soden's work is its unintentional confirmation of the work of WH. Although von Soden proceeded from a radically different theory than that of WH, the result was a text which was not radically different from the WH text and which equally rejected the TR.

D. CURRENT VIEW OF LOCAL TEXTS

1. The Alexandrian Text

Further studies have indicated that WH were somewhat too optimistic in their designation of a "Neutral" text. The agreement of B ℵ remains one of the most highly regarded witnesses to the NT text, but it is generally doubted that the text is as pure as WH believed it to be. Together with the modification of the view of WH has come the conclusion that the WH "Alexandrian" text is not a text distinct from the "Neutral"; rather, that the

---

[4]For details see Lake, pp. 89–90, or Kenyon, *Handbook*, pp. 52–55.
[5]Benedikt Kraft, *Die Zeichen für die wichtigeren Handschriften des griechischen Neuen Testaments*, 3d ed. Freiburg: Herder, 1955.

"Alexandrian" witnesses represent perhaps slightly differing degrees of fidelity to the same text to which B א belong. As a result, it is now common to combine both of these WH texts under the designation of "Alexandrian." As such, it is probably the best single text of the local texts; but like the others its readings cannot be accepted uncritically but must be submitted to the principles of criticism.

The Alexandrian text is more likely to be wrong in the more "sophisticated" variants—e.g., those involving technicalities of grammar or those in which a more literary form is substituted for a more colloquial form. An example of the former type may be one which occurs in 2 Cor. 7:14; here the original text may be ἐπὶ Τίτου, which could be construed either as "our boasting in Titus became true" or "our boasting became true in Titus," and the reading ἡ ἐπί Τίτου, an Alexandrian addition to ensure the former meaning. In Phil. 2:11, similarly, ἐξομολογήσεται is probably original and intended to be the second verb in the ἵνα clause, but it could be interpreted as the verb of a separate clause ("and, indeed, every tongue shall confess"); the Alexandrian change to ἐξομολογήσηται gives the more correct form for a verb of a ἵνα clause and also ensures that it will not be interpreted as a separate clause. In Rom. 15:26 and 15:27 some good Alexandrian witnesses have probably substituted the more classical augmented form ηὐδόκησαν for the original εὐδόκησαν, the usual NT form.

On the other hand, the Alexandrian text retains original readings which are terse or somewhat rough, and readings which are superficially more difficult but which commend themselves on further study: e.g., λέγω ὑμῖν ἀπέχουσιν instead of λέγω ὑμῖν ὅτι ἀπέχουσιν in Matt. 6:16, προσέχετε instead of προσέχετε δέ in Matt. 7:15, ἐν αὐτῷ in John 3:15 ("might have eternal life in him"), and μονογενὴς θεός in John 1:18.

2. The Western Text

The Western text is often unique among the text-types. It has its share of readings which call for no more comment than many readings found in other text-types, including many readings which it has in combination with other texts. Yet there are numerous readings which are sufficiently unusual as to be set apart from other variants, consisting of long additions to the ordinary text. These are especially characteristic of the Western text of Acts, but are found to some extent elsewhere in the NT. One such long addition occurs at the end of Acts 6:10 and another at the beginning of Luke 6:5; a long paraphrase occurs in Acts 11:2; and numerous others may be noted in a critical apparatus.

The Western text also substitutes synonyms for single words, such as ἔνεγκε instead of εἰσάγαγε in Luke 14:21 and αἰνοῦντες instead of εὐλογοῦντες in Luke 24:53; it makes slight changes in meaning, such as ἑπταπλασίονα instead of πολλαπλασίονα in Luke 18:30, and αὐτοῦ instead of αὐτοί ("we have heard him" instead of "we ourselves have heard") in John 4:42. The Western text also makes minor revisions, such as the addition of ὑμῶν, ταῦτα after πατρός in John 8:38 and the substitution of τὴν γῆν for γῆς in Mark 4:5.

Most puzzling are numerous instances in which the Western text has a reading which is shorter than the alternative readings, since shorter readings are generally considered preferable (if an intentional variation is indicated); and yet the Western text is not generally preferred when it stands alone. One group of these shorter Western readings is found in the latter part of Luke: e.g., the omission of the second half of Luke 23:39, the omission of the first sentence of Luke 24:6, and the omissions of ἐν ταῖς ἡμέραις ἐκείναις, of καὶ προφητεύσουσιν, and of αἷμα καὶ πῦρ καὶ ἀτμίδα καπνοῦ, all in Acts 2:18–19.

Those who accepted the conclusions of WH largely tended to dismiss the Western text as corrupt. WH themselves, however, had recognized that the Western text could be traced back to the second century, which meant that it was attested at a date earlier than any other text. They likewise believed that shorter readings in the Western text, "Western non-interpolations," deserved special consideration. At the same time, they felt that no reading with solely Western support could be accepted as original without serious question.

Shortly after Westcott and Hort published their work, scholars began to turn their attention to a serious study of the Western text, perhaps in part deliberately and in part being drawn
to it by studies of the text of ancient versions and Fathers. This
study followed a number of different lines. One branch devoted
itself to Codex Bezae (Codex D of the Gospels and Acts), which
was virtually the only uncial Greek witness to the Western text
of the Gospels and Acts. Other studies were concerned with the
Old Latin and still others wih the Old Syriac, both of which are
witnesses to the Western text. The NT text quoted by Cyprian
and certain other early Fathers was likewise found to be a Western text.

Theories of the origin of the Western text were various.
Westcott-Hort considered it to have arisen as a deliberate second-
century revision. Others tried to explain it as the result of re-
translation into Greek from Syriac or from the Old Latin,
perhaps to make the Greek agree with the Syriac or the Old
Latin in a bilingual MS. Since the most striking elements of the
Western text occur in Luke and Acts, a few scholars theorized
that Luke had himself issued two editions of Luke and Acts, one
somewhat longer than the other, the longer edition being the
Western text. (There was difference of opinion as to whether
the longer or the shorter was the first edition.) A. C. Clark, a
classical scholar, accustomed to finding accidental omissions
rather than intentional additions in the texts of the classics,
maintained that the longer Western text of Luke and Acts was
original and that the shorter forms were the result of accidental
(in his first books) or intentional (in his latest book) omissions.

Numerous theories have thus been proposed to explain the
origin of the Western text, but the final answer seems to be as
much shrouded in mystery as ever. It now appears that the
Western text may be divided into three subgroups, with Codex
D representing one group, the Old Latin MSS *k* and *e* a second
group, and the Old Syriac a third group.

The study of the Western text continues, and articles dealing
with this text frequently appear in the scholarly journals. At

present, while some scholars have a relatively high opinion of the Western text, most scholars find that upon examination of individual readings those with only Western support generally do not commend themselves upon the principles of internal evidence.

3. The Caesarean Text

One of the significant developments in textual studies in the present century has been the identification of a local text which was unknown both to WH and to von Soden. In 1868 W. H. Ferrar discovered that Codex 13 and three other minuscules were so closely related as to constitute a "family" (now known as Family 13 or the Ferrar Group). In 1902 Kirsopp Lake showed that a group of minuscules headed by Codex 1 formed a "family" (Family 1) and that this family was in turn textually similar to that of Family 13 and to the minuscules 28, 565, and 700. In 1913 Beerman and Gregory published the text of the uncial Codex Θ, and in 1923 Lake and others showed that this MS fell into the company of Family 1 and its relatives. B. H. Streeter pointed out that Origen used this text-type at Caesarea and therefore designated it the "Caesarean text." Soon afterward he added the text of Mark (except for the first five chapters) in Codex W to the Caesarean witnesses. In 1928 Lake and his co-workers added Eusebius, the Old Georgian, the Old Armenian, and the Palestinian Syriac to the Caesarean witnesses, at least in Mark. The Chester Beatty Papyrus of the Gospels ($\mathfrak{P}^{45}$) was added to these witnesses after its text was published in 1934. It was then suggested that there were two principal subdivisions of the Caesarean text, the one consisting of $\mathfrak{P}^{45}$, W, f^1, f^{13}, and 28, and the other including Θ, 565, and 700. In 1947, in his doctoral dissertation, the present writer established Cyril of Jerusalem as a strong Caesarean witness in the Gospels.[6]

The Caesarean text lies mid-way, so to speak, between the Alexandrian and the Western text. It may be slightly closer to the Western, but it does not generally include the long additions and long paraphrases of the Western text or the long addi-

---

[6]Published in 1955 as *Studies and Documents XVII*.

tions of the TR. It is often found in the company of the Alexandrian text (e.g., χριστὸν εἶναι in Mark 1:34), often with the Western text (e.g., ἵνα βλέποντες μή βλέπωσιν in Matt. 13:13), and often with its own readings apart from the other local texts (e.g., καὶ before μὴ in John 2:16). Its use by Cyril of Jerusalem indicates that it was the text of more than Caesarea—perhaps it is the "Palestinian" text; but the designation of "Caesarean" has become established, and there is not sufficient reason to change it, since the designations of the other texts are now also recognized to be somewhat arbitrary.

4. The Byzantine Text

The Syrian text of WH has likewise been the subject of investigation, both by von Soden and by later scholars. Since the term "Syrian" is subject to confusion with the Syriac version, this text was sometimes designated the Antiochene, for the Syrian city of Antioch; it is now generally called the Byzantine, for Byzantium (Constantinople).

It is generally agreed that some of the later uncial MSS, most of the minuscules, and the later versions and Fathers represent a late text which is inferior to the other text-types. Of course, many Byzantine readings are supported by other evidence and are good readings. It is likewise possible that in some instances the true reading has been lost from the MSS of the other text-types and is preserved only in the Byzantine text. For this reason Byzantine readings must not automatically be rejected without examination. At the same time, the general impression given by readings that are characteristically Byzantine is that they are inferior and not likely to be original.

Byzantine readings are characteristically smooth, clear, and full. A conjunction or an appropriate word may be added to smooth out a rough transition (e.g., in Mark 2:16, adding τί before ὅτι μετά). The text may be changed to clarify a meaning (Mark 7:5, ἀνίπτοις for κοιναίς; Mark 5:14, τοὺς χοιρούς for αὐτούς; Mark 5:13, the addition of εὐθέως ὁ Ἰησοῦς after ἐπέτρεψεν). A difficulty of meaning or a reading harder to understand may be alleviated (Mark 1:2, τοῖς προφήταις instead of τῷ Ἠσαΐᾳ τῷ προφήτῃ; Matt. 11:2, δύο for διά; John 12:7, τετήρηκεν instead of ἵνα τηρήσῃ). The theology or the meaning in general may be strengthened (Matt. 6:4, the addition of ἐν τῷ φανερῷ to give added emphasis to the reward and to balance the preceding ἐν τῷ κρυπτῷ; Acts 2:1, ὁμοθυμαδόν instead of the more neutral ὁμοῦ; and possibly 1 Tim. 3:16, θεός for ὅς). Sometimes two separate readings are combined (Mark 6:33, προῆλθον αὐτοὺς καὶ συνῆλθον πρὸς αὐτόν; Mark 9:49, πᾶς γὰρ πυρὶ ἁλισθήσεται καὶ πᾶσα θυσία ἅλι ἁλισθήσεται; Luke 24:53, εὐλογοῦντες καὶ αἰνοῦντες). One of the most common characteristics of the Byzantine text is the harmonization of parallel passages (e.g., harmonization of the shorter form of the Lord's Prayer in Luke 11:2–4 to the longer form in Matt. 6:9–13; and the addition of ἡ φυγὴ ὑμῶν from Matt. 24:20 to Mark 13:18).

E. Numeration of Greek Manuscripts

As the early period of NT textual criticism progressed, it became necessary to designate the MSS in some manner which would not be too cumbersome for citation in a critical apparatus. Wettstein had initiated the practice of designating uncial MSS by capital letters and minuscule MSS by arabic numbers, but even this system had become complicated. If a MSS contained only the Gospels, then another MSS containing, for example, the Pauline epistles might be assigned the same letter or number. Still more confusing was the related fact that a MS which contained most of the NT often received different designations in different parts of the NT. For example, the famous Codex 33 was known as 33 in the Gospels, 13 in Acts and the Catholic Epistles, and 17 in the Pauline epistles. In addition, various other designations were in use for other MSS: different sets of arabic numbers, lower-case letters, and numerous other types of abbreviations. When C. R. Gregory prepared the volume of prolegomena for Tischendorf's eighth major edition of the NT he included a tremendous amount of helpful information concerning the known Greek MSS as well as other witnesses, including some cross-referencing of the number of the same MS in different parts of the NT. Later he devoted a separate volume to the establishment of a unified nomenclature for all papyri, uncials, and minuscules then known, and to a complete cross-reference between the older systems of designation and his new system. This volume, *Die griechischen Handschriften des NT*, published in 1908, is virtually indispensable for exhaustive textual work, although it is out of print and can rarely be purchased; but it is usually found in well-equipped biblical libraries. This work has been brought up to date, although with less cross-referencing of the various systems of numeration, by Kurt Aland's *Kurzgefaßte Liste der griechischen Handschriften des Neuen Testaments*.

Most textual studies since the introduction of Gregory's system of numbering have followed the new designations. On the other hand, Tischendorf followed the older systems, of course, which means that virtually every reference to a minuscule MS outside the Gospels must be changed to the Gregory number, and many MSS designations even in the Gospels must likewise be translated, for use in present-day work.

Gregory's system of numbering has been a great contribution to textual study. It soon became the regular custom for newly discovered MSS to be reported for addition to this list, which has now become recognized as the official international catalog of MSS. With the death of Gregory in the First World War the catalog passed into the keeping of another German scholar. This responsibility was later passed to Prof. Kurt Aland, and, following his death in 1994, to his widow, Barbara Aland.

F. SIGNIFICANT MODERN EDITIONS OF THE GREEK NEW TESTAMENT

Tischendorf's eighth major edition, in two volumes plus a volume of introductory material, was published in 1869, 1872, and 1894 respectively. Its text leans a bit too heavily on Codex ℵ. The apparatus contains a wealth of information and is essential to anyone doing extensive textual work.

Von Soden's edition was published in 1913. The text is a critical text constructed on principles quite different from that of WH. The apparatus cites more Greek minuscules than does Tischendorf, but the versions and the Fathers are rather neglected. The apparatus, moreover, is presented in a complicated and confusing manner.

An exhaustive two-volume edition of Revelation was published by H. C. Hoskier in 1929. Hoskier prints the TR and attempts in his apparatus to cite completely every Greek MS of Revelation known to him, plus some versions and Fathers. He uses a different numeration, however, developed by F. H. A. Scrivener, which makes it necessary to translate his numbers into Gregory numbers. Hoskier furnishes a cross-reference list for this purpose.

Since much new material had become available after the publication of Tischendorf's final edition, a project was undertaken in England to prepare a new edition on a similarly exhaustive scale, of which Mark was published in 1935 and Matthew in 1940 under the editorship of S. C. E. Legg. Luke was also completed in manuscript form when the project was discontinued because the edition seemed unsatisfactory in some respects. The text printed is that of WH; and the apparatus, although it contains some defects, contains a considerable amount of information not found in Tischendorf. Most students, however, will depend largely on one or more small-size editions.

The Greek NT sponsored by the United Bible Societies (1st ed., 1966; 4th revised ed., 1993–94) was unique in being prepared by a committee rather than by one or two persons. The text, originally the result of the committee's decisions, has now been made identical with the 26th and 27th editions of the Nestle-Aland text. Beginning with the Third "Corrected" Edition, the punctuation was conformed to the German punctuation of the Nestle-Aland text as well, which is sometimes different from American style and can be confusing.

The critical apparatus is intended to be limited to variants which are significant for Bible students and translators. The witnesses are cited in detail, which makes this NT the best for beginning students of textual criticism. In the fourth edition, the critical apparatus for numerous variants was dropped and an approximately equal number of new variants were added. There are still, however, many bracketed words or phrases with no critical apparatus.

In the fourth edition the punctuation apparatus has been expanded to include differences on section, paragraph, and clause level as well, as found in various Greek and modern language editions. The apparatus of cross references is helpful in indicating the specific part of verses referred to.

The series of editions originated by Eberhard Nestle in 1898 is now edited by Barbara Aland. The text was originally based on the agreement of the majority of the texts of Tischendorf, WH, and Weiss, but recent editions have depended more on the editor's decisions. The apparatus is concise but helpful.

In 1910 Alexander Souter published a Greek NT, of which a revised edition was issued in 1947. The text is intended to represent the Greek text behind the English Revised NT of 1881 and is therefore not Souter's own critical text. The apparatus deals with far fewer variants than do the other common small editions, but gives extensive evidence from the versions and the Fathers in the variants which are dealt with.

Two Greek and Latin editions prepared by Roman Catholic scholars are somewhat similar to each other. The tenth edition of Merk's NT appeared in 1984, and the sixth edition of Bover was published in 1981. Both of these editions have critical texts that are somewhat influenced by von Soden's text and by the Vulgate. Their apparatuses cite witnesses in much greater detail than does Nestle, and they cite many minuscules.

The fourth edition of Vogel's Greek and Latin NT was published in 1955. This Roman Catholic scholar's text seems to be closer to both von Soden and the TR than are the other critical texts which have been mentioned. The apparatus is quite limited, both in the number of variants dealt with and in the extent of the evidence cited. A surprising and inconvenient feature of the apparatus is its citation of minuscule MSS by the symbols used by Tischendorf, which, especially outside the Gospels, must be changed to Gregory numbers for use in textual work.

While the Nestle editions were continuing to be issued, the British and Foreign Bible Society had continued to distribute the fourth edition since 1904. This edition indicated alternate readings but had no true critical apparatus. In 1958 the BFBS published a slightly revised text with a brief critical apparatus, edited by G. D. Kilpatrick, a well-known Oxford NT scholar. This edition was designated the BFBS second edition.

Chapter 7

❦

THE PRAXIS OF TEXTUAL CRITICISM

A. HOW TO READ A CRITICAL APPARATUS

Before studying some specific examples of textual variants it will be well to become acquainted with the critical apparatus of the commonly used editions of the Greek NT. These will be discussed in the order in which a student may find it convenient to use them—beginning with the Bible Societies' text, then Nestle and other pocket editions, and finally the larger editions.

1. The Bible Societies' Greek New Testament (4th Revised Ed.)

a. Manner of Citation. The introduction to this edition describes these matters in detail. A superscript sequential number identifies the variant, followed by the verse number in which it is found. Then, within braces, a letter, A, B, C, or D, indicates the Editorial Committee's degree of certainty concerning the reading of the text. Then follows the indication of the text chosen, with its support, followed by other readings with their support. (Double-bracketed passages such as John 7:53–8:11 may have the witnesses against the bracketed text first.)

b. Symbols Used. "Byz" means that the reading is supported by the later witnesses in general which constitute the Byzantine text. "Lect" indicates the consensus of the lectionaries. An asterisk (*) following a MS designation (e.g., C*) means that this is the original reading but that an alteration has occurred; the alteration ("successive correctors") is indicated by a superscript letter or numeral (e.g., C³, Bᶜ). Specific MSS of the Old Latin are indicated by superscript letters, and of the Vulgate by superscript syllables. Individual versions of the Syriac, and portions of other versions, are similarly indicated.

2. Nestle-Aland, 27th ed.

a. Manner of Citation. Instead of indicating the location of a variant by quoting Nestle's text in the critical apparatus, Nestle-Aland uses a series of symbols in the body of the text to indicate various types of variants. The same symbol is then given in the apparatus to identify the variant with the text. If the same symbol must be used more than once within a given verse, the subsequent symbols are distinguished by a point or by a numeral following. (See the card which accompanies Nestle's text, and Nestle-Aland 27th, p. 52*.)

Alternative readings, followed by their evidence, are given, with the readings separated by the symbol ¦. If Nestle's text itself is given, it is given last. Often Nestle's text is not given, the assumption being that evidence not otherwise cited supports Nestle's text. If a cited MS is enclosed in parentheses, it indicates that this MS supports the reading for which it is cited rather than the other reading(s) cited, but in a form slightly different from the reading as cited.

Nestle frequently indicates the reading of the text of various editors. In such instances, a semicolon (;) follows the citation of evidence for a reading, then the initials of the editors are given. (See pp. 82*–83* of Nestle-Aland 27th for the key to these initials.)

An internal variant within a given reading is enclosed in parentheses, together with the evidence and citation of editors.

Evidence is cited in the following order: papyri, uncials, minuscules, versions, Fathers.

b. Symbols Used. Through the 25th ed., the letter 𝕾 indicated the consensus of the Alexandrian (i.e., "Hesychian") witnesses, and the letter 𝕶 the Byzantine (i.e., "Koine") witnesses. (See pp. 15*–16*, 68*–69* of Nestle 25th and the card accompanying the text for a list of the witnesses included in these groups.) The minuscule Family 1 was indicated by the letter λ (for "Lake"), and Family 13 by φ (for "Ferrar"). Beginning with the 26th ed., the principal Alexandrian witnesses are cited individually, the consensus of the Byzantine witnesses is indicated by the letter 𝔐, and Families 1 and 13 are indicated by italic f^1 and f^{13} respectively.

An asterisk indicates the original reading of a MS at a point where there is also a correction or change. Correctors are indicated by e.g., C**, C^c, B^2, etc.

A period following cited evidence means that there is no other evidence known to Nestle which supports this reading (e.g., Mark 5:38).

Versions are indicated by non-capitalized abbreviations. (See Nestle-Aland 27th, pp. 63*–72*, for details.)

Church fathers are indicated by abbreviations with initial capitals. (See Nestle-Aland 27th, pp. 72*–76*, for details.)

An italic p preceding a reading in the critical apparatus means that this is the approximate reading of a parallel passage (e.g., Mark 5:36). Occasionally, the actual reference to the passage from which a reading may have come will be given (e.g., in Luke 1:3).

A "conjecture"—a reading proposed apart from any textual evidence—is indicated by the italic cj, usually accompanied by the name of the person who first proposed the conjecture (e.g., Mark 1:2–3).

An exclamation mark (!) preceding a reading indicates that Nestle believes that this reading may be the original even though it is not the reading of his text (e.g., John 1:18).

To illustrate the use of Nestle's apparatus by an example, the data concerning a variant in Matt. 22:44 would be read as follows in the 27th edition: In v. 44, the article ὁ is present before κύριος in L W Θ f^1 f^{13} 33, a few other MSS, and the Byzantine witnesses represented by 𝔐. Nestle's text (i.e., which omits the article) is supported by ℵ B D Z.

The inner margins of the Gospels contain a series of two sets of numbers, the lower of which is a roman numeral. The upper numbers, which are in sequence, are the ancient Ammonian sections, dividing each Gospel into sections or paragraphs. Many ancient MSS of the Gospels contain these sections (in Greek letter-numerals), and students who study these MSS will find these section numbers helpful in locating passages in them. The lower numbers refer to the Eusebian Canons on pp. 85*–89*, which indicate parallels in the other Gospels for each section.

3. BFBS Second Edition (Kilpatrick)

The apparatus to this edition is largely self-explanatory. The few symbols and abbreviations used are explained on pp. vii–ix, xiv–xxi, xxiii.

To illustrate with an example, the data concerning the variant in Matt. 22:44 would be read as follows:

> In v. 44, the BFBS text reads Κυριος supported by ℵ B D Z. No other witnesses of any kind support this reading (this is indicated by the period at the end of the evidence). The alternative reading, which is the form of the text of Ps. 110:1, is ο Κυριος, which is supported by the rest of the witnesses. It is also the reading of the TR and of the English Revised version of 1881.

4. Souter

a. Manner of Citation. The first reading given in the critical apparatus is the reading of Souter's text.

The textual evidence for each reading is given following the reading (see at Mark 1:1). If only a small amount of the evidence supports the alternative reading, evidence may be given not for the first reading, but only for the alternate reading, the assumption being that the evidence not specifically cited for the alternate reading supports the first reading—the reading of Souter's text (see at Mark 1:41).

If evidence is given for the first reading, a colon (:) stands at the end of this evidence to separate it from the second reading, and likewise to separate any additional readings. If evidence is not given for the first reading, a square bracket (]) separates this reading from the second reading. An observable space separates the readings of one variant from the readings of the next variant (see the three variants in Mark 1:13).[1]

Sometimes Souter wishes to indicate an internal variation within a given reading. A word or words enclosed in square brackets within a reading indicates that that part of the reading is omitted by some of the evidence cited for the reading (see at Mark 1:2). Other internal variations, such as different words or word order, are given in parentheses (see Mark 1:29, third reading). Sometimes the specific evidence supporting this internal variant is given within the parentheses (see at Mark 1:1). If a cited MS is enclosed in brackets (see at Mark 1:27, last reading) or in parentheses (see at Mark 5:1), it indicates that the MS thus enclosed supports the reading in a slightly different form but still can be cited in support of the reading given rather than one of the other alternatives. Evidence is cited in the following order: papyri, uncials, minuscules, versions, Fathers.

b. Symbols Used. The minuscule MSS groups Family 1 and Family 13 are written "1 &c." and "13 &c." (see Souter, p. xii, for further details concerning these families).

An asterisk (e.g., C*) denotes the original reading of a MS at a point where there is also a correction or change (the correction indicated by C**, Cᶜ, C², etc.; see Souter, p. x).

The lower-case *omega* (ω) does not refer to a particular MS, but indicates the reading of the consensus of the minuscule MSS.

The principal versions are indicated by gothic letters, with more specific identification given within parentheses following (for details, see Souter, pp. xviii–xx). Note that if the gothic letter itself is in parentheses, it indicates that the version differs slightly from the wording of the reading for which is it cited, as in the case of Greek MSS (see at Mark 7:3); however, the specific

---

[1] Unfortunately, there are occasional errors in the apparatus in this respect: e.g., in Mark 1:2 a colon, not a space, should precede the words εν τοις προφηταις; and there should be no bracket immediately following την οδον σου in Mark 1:2 or following αυτον in Mark 1:34.

versions indicated following the gothic letter are always in parentheses, and this does not indicate any such variation.

Church fathers are cited by abbreviations of their names (see Souter, pp. xxi–xxv). When a fraction appears following the name of a Father, the lower number indicates the total number of times the Father quotes the passage, and the upper number indicates the number of those times when he quotes the passage in the form for which he is cited in support; e.g., in Mark 1:1 the Latin version of Irenaeus quotes the passage three times, twice including υιου του θεου and once omitting these words.

Souter gives a list of the Latin words whose abbreviations he uses (pp. xxvii f.). For the English meaning of some of these Latin terms, see the Appendix of the present book.

To illustrate the use of Souter's critical apparatus by an example, the data concerning the variant in Matt. 22:38 would be read as follows:

> In v. 38, where the text reads η μεγαλη και πρωτη, this reading (with or without the η) is supported by ℵ B D L Z Θ fam. 1 fam. 13 700, the Latin versions (Itala and Vulgate), the Old Syriac (Curetonian and Sinaitic), Peshitta, the Palestinian Syriac, the Sahidic and Bohairic versions, and the Ethiopic. The reading πρωτη και η μεγαλη (with or without η) is supported by W, the minuscules in general, three MSS of the Itala (d f q), the Harkleian Syriac, and the Armenian version. The reading η πρωτη alone is supported by the Latin Father Ambrosiaster.

5. Merk

a. Manner of Citation. Merk has organized the witnesses which he cites into groupings resembling von Soden's system. These groups differ in various sections of the NT. His Gospels groups, for example, are *H, D, C, K,* and *Comment. in J.* The *C* and *K* groups are further subdivided, the subgroups designated by Greek or English letters.

Merk cites witnesses in the order they appear in his textual grouping. The group and subgroup in which Merk places a given MS can be located by referring to his index of MSS.

Care must be taken to refer to the proper list of the various sections of the NT: Gospels, Acts, Pauline epistles (including Hebrews), Catholic Epistles, and Revelation.

The first reading in the critical apparatus is usually the reading of Merk's text. Sometimes, however, if the evidence is to be given for the alternate reading only and if this alternate reading rather closely resembles the reading of Merk's text, the apparatus will merely give the alternate reading and its evidence (e.g., Mark 1:24).

Unless otherwise indicated, alternate readings are alternatives to the first reading *in its entirety.*

If evidence is given for only one reading, the assumption is that the remaining evidence supports the other reading (e.g., both variants in Mark 1:28).

An internal variant within a reading may be indicated by parentheses (e.g., Mark 1:1). A MS in parentheses indicates support for the cited reading but in a slightly differing form (e.g., Mark 1:34, end).

b. Symbols Used. Codex ℵ is designated Codex S, and the Gregory Codex S is Codex 028. Codex 046 is cited as Codex Q.

A vertical line (|) indicates the end of a variant.

A square bracket ( ]) indicates the end of a reading and its evidence.

A horizontal caret (⟩) indicates an omission, either of the previous reading (e.g., Mark 1:1) or of the word(s) following (e.g., Mark 1:5, παντες).

A lower-case *s* on the line (e.g., "348s" in Mark 1:2) refers to the MS which follows the previously cited MS in Merk's groupings. Additional MSS following are indicated by *ss* or *sss*. For example, in Mark 1:2, "348s" means MSS 348 and 1279; in Mark 1:16 "579ss" means 579 Δ 1241.

A small superscript *s* means that most of the MSS from the MS previously cited to the end of that subgroup (i.e., to the next vertical line) support the reading referred to. For example, in Mark 1:17, 1424^s includes the MSS of the Cφ^a class (from 1424 through 1188).

A superscript r means that most of the MSS from the immediately preceding MS to the end of the *entire family* (D, C$_\eta$, K$^\kappa$,
etc.) support the reading referred to. For example, in Mark 1:45,
7^r includes the MSS of the Cφ family from 7 through 692.

When two MSS are connected by a hyphen (-), it indicates
that these two MSS and most of the MSS between them in Merk's
list support the reading. For example, in Mark 1:34 W-28 includes W Θ 700 372 565 28; and 1-1082 includes most MSS from
1 (in Cη^a) through 1082 (in Cφ^b).

In the above paragraphs, if a Gospel or Gospels (or other
books in other sections of the NT) are named in Merk's groups,
it means that the MS preceding this designation is to be counted
in the sequence of MSS only in the book or books indicated by
the abbreviation. For example, in Merk's groupings for the Gospels ("Codices Evangeliorum"), Ψ is to be included in the *H*
group in Mark, Luke, and John only; Z is to be included in the *H*
group in Matthew only; 067 is to be included in the Ca group in
Matthew and Mark only; etc.

It is important to note that the superscript s and r do not
make it certain that *every* MS included within the designation
supports the reading referred to. It is therefore not safe to
cite *any* single MS thus included, since one may assume only
that *most* of the MSS support the reading; and it cannot be determined which, if any, are excluded. For the same reason,
when two MSS are connected by a hyphen it is safe to assume
that *every* MS between the two supports the same reading
only if there are *not more than four* MSS intervening between
the two.

The abbreviation *rel.* following a MS means that most of the
MSS from the one just named to the end of Merk's entire list
support the reading referred to (e.g., Mark 12:26); *rel.* with no
MS preceding means most of the MSS not cited for other readings
(e.g., Mark 13:35); *rel. pl.* refers to most of the remaining MSS.

The symbol ~ means that the following reading is a change
of word order from the previous reading or from Merk's text
(e.g., Mark 1:45).

The abbreviation *pr.* means that the following word(s) are to be "prefixed to" (i.e., placed before) the word(s) of the previous reading (e.g., John 8:25).

A hyphen (-) separating two words of a reading in the apparatus means that the reading includes all of Merk's text from the first word through the second word thus given (e.g., Mark 2:10).

Sometimes it is necessary to assume what the ending is for a word given in the apparatus. For example, in Mark 2:16 the first reading is των φαρισ., which is of course the των φαρισαιων of Merk's text. The alternate reading is given as κ. οι φαρ. Here κ. must be assumed to mean και, and φαρ. must be assumed to have the ending which would agree with οι—hence, οι φαρισαιοι.

The abbreviation *inc.* means that the reading which follows is an alternate reading for the beginning (*incipit*) of the verse. It is assumed that the reader can tell how much of the beginning of Merk's text is substituted by this alternate reading (e.g., in Mark 2:27 λεγω δε υμιν οτι is presumably an alternate reading for the και ελεγεν αυτοις of Merk's text).

The symbol ⌒ indicates an omission which Merk assumes is due to homoioteleuton. For example, in Mark 4:37 πλοιον1 ⌒ 2 means that the witnesses following have skipped from the first occurrence of πλοιον to the second occurrence, omitting the words ωστε ηδη γεμιζεσθαι το πλοιον.

A biblical reference accompanying a reading indicates the passage from which the present reading may have developed (e.g., Mark 3:2).

In the MSS of Revelation, a small superscript *2* at the beginning of a number indicates 2000; e.g., [2]51 means MS 2051.

Merk commonly cites editors in support of readings, using an initial letter for each editor (see the introduction). Editors are cited immediately following the reading and are separated from the citation of MSS by a colon (:).

Versions are indicated by abbreviations. Church fathers are likewise indicated by abbreviations.

To illustrate by an example, the data concerning the variant in Matt. 22:38 would be read as follows:

In v. 38, μεγαλη και πρωτη, the reading of the text, is supported by the Arabic and Venetian Gospel harmonies which are possibly related to the work of Tatian, by all or almost all of the MSS of the *H* text from B through 892 of Merk's list (i.e., B ℵ C Z 33 L 892), by D Θ, by all or most of the MSS of the C$_η$ family (1 through 131), by most mss of the C$_ι$ family (13 through 124), by 1093, by much of the Latin (Itala and Vulgate), the Old Syriac (Curetonian and Sinaitic), the Peshitta, the Palestinian Syriac, the Armenian, the Georgian, and the Coptic (Sahidic and Bohairic) versions. The alternative word order πρωτη και μεγαλη is supported by Irenaeus, Ephraem, and the remaining witnesses in general.

6. Bover

a. Manner of Citation. Bover's presentation of MSS evidence is quite similar to that of Merk. His groupings of MSS are similar (see the introduction and the card accompanying the text). Bover, however, divides the NT into only three sections, placing Acts, Paul and Hebrews, and the Catholic Epistles into one group and indicating by a superscript letter if a witness is to be included in only part of this group (e.g., Codex M is to be included in the *H* group in Paul only). Moreover, Bover's list of MSS gives no key to the location of a MS in his groups, although Merk's index may be of help for Bover's listings as well.

b. Symbols Used. Bover's symbols are similar to those used by Merk, with some exceptions. Omissions are indicated by the abbreviation *om.* Two words separated by ellipses (. . .) indicate that the reading extends from the first word through the second word thus quoted (e.g., Luke 9:62). Several symbols used by Merk are not used by Bover.

When a variant deals with a change of word order, if more than two words are involved, Bover often indicates where the transposition occurs by inserting a diagonal line (/) in the first reading; then he merely uses the symbol ~ for the second reading without quoting the words (e.g., in Mark 4:32 the second reading will be παντων των λαχανων μειζον.

A citation such as "𝔓⁴⁵ . . . " means that 𝔓⁴⁵ and most other MSS not elsewhere cited in the readings support this reading (e.g., Luke 10:15).

In some minor variants, such as alternate spellings, Bover cites editors but no MSS or other witnesses (e.g., Luke 9:36).

To illustrate by an example, the data concerning the variant in Matt. 22:44 in Bover's critical apparatus would be read as follows:

> In v. 44, the article ὁ before κυριος, which is Bover's text, is included in von Soden's NT in brackets and is the text of Vogels and Merk; it is supported in general by the witnesses which are not cited for the alternate reading. The alternate reading, which is the omission of the article ὁ, is the reading of the texts of Tischendorf, Wescott-Hort, Weiss, LaGrange, and von Soden's alternative to his bracketed text; this reading is supported by B ℵ Z D.

7. Legg (published for Matthew and Mark only)

a. Manner of Citation. Legg does not classify the witnesses into groups. He gives uncials, papyri, minuscules, lectionaries, versions, and Fathers in that order, with the Greek MSS given in alphabetical or numerical order. He uses the Gregory numeration throughout. A brief identification of principal witnesses cited is given at the beginning of the volume.

A note in parentheses following a witness refers to the single witness immediately preceding the parenthesis; e.g., in Mark 1:1 Legg indicates that the original hand of Codex 28 omits χριστου and the Palestinian Syriac prefixes "Lord" (κυριου, indicated by the Latin *domini*) and hence reads the equivalent of κυριου Ιησου Χριστου.

b. Symbols Used. The Hebrew letter ל includes the reading of the Byzantine-text uncials E F G H K M S U V Y Ω.

A colon (:) is placed at the end of the evidence for the first reading given in the apparatus (which is Legg's text, the text of WH). If more than one alternate reading is given, these alternative readings may be separated by a semicolon (;).

The symbol ⟩ indicates that the following reading is a change of word order (e.g., Mark 3:12).

The symbol ~ indicates that only the last part of a word is changed in the following reading (e.g., in Mark 1:10, instead of καταβαινον, Codex D*—the original hand of D—and certain other MSS read καταβαινων, and Codex Ω reads καταπαινων).

The minuscule families 1 and 13 are indicated as fam.[1] and fam.[13] respectively.

The symbol + indicates an addition to the preceding reading (e.g., Mark 1:38, αυτοις: + ο Ιησους). In Mark 1:13, + και τεσσ. ημερας is an addition to the first reading, τεσσ. ημερας, not an addition to the changed word order > ημερας τεσσ.

The symbol = does not necessarily mean "equals" and may sometimes be disregarded, as in Mark 1:1.

The meaning of some of the Latin terms used by Legg may be found in the Appendix of the present book.

To illustrate the use of Legg's critical apparatus by an example, the data concerning the second variant in Mark 1:1 would be read as follows:

> Ιησου Χριστου with nothing further in the sentence, which is the reading of Legg's (WH) text, is supported by the original text of ℵ, by Θ 28 (but the original of 28 omits Χριστου) 255, the original of 1555, by the Palestinian Syriac (which actually reads "Lord Jesus Christ"), the Adysh MS of the Georgian version, and nine MSS of the Armenian; a similar reading but probably not identical is supported by eight Fathers; a similar reading is likewise supported by marginal notes in MSS 237 238 259. A second reading, Ιησου Χριστου υιου θεου, is supported by a corrector of ℵ and by B D L W. A slightly different reading, Ιησου Χριστου υιου του θεου, is supported by A Γ Δ Π Σ Φ and eleven other uncials, and by the minuscules other than those cited previously. Similarly, "Jesus Christ Son of God" (it is not possible to distinguish between θεου and του θεου in these witnesses) is supported by the Old Latin, by the Vulgate (although three MSS of the Vulgate read "our Lord Jesus Christ Son of God"), the Peshitta and Harkleian Syriac, the Sahidic and Bohairic, the Athos and Leningrad MSS of the Georgian, an edition of the Armenian which is based upon three of the best Armenian MSS, and the Ethiopic; a similar reading is supported by five Fathers (including Origen's works translated into Latin) and other unnamed Fathers; "Son of God" (omitting "Jesus Christ") is supported often by the works of Irenaeus; and Epiphanius has a still different reading which is given by Legg at the bottom of the page (this reading omits the entire name and title of Jesus).

8. Tischendorf[2]

a. Manner of Citation. The first reading given in the apparatus by Tischendorf is that of his own text. The agreement of the text of certain editors is indicated by an abbreviation of the editor's name either before or following a reading (e.g., Griesbach, Scholz, Lachmann).[3] Then follows *c.* or *cum* ("with") followed by the evidence for the first reading. For example, in Mark 9:3 the apparatus indicates that Tischendorf's text reads εγενετο with the support of א B C E F and certain other MSS, while εγενοντο is read by Lachmann, Tischendorf's 7th ed., and MSS A D G K L and others.

The witnesses are cited in the following order: uncials, minuscules, including lectionaries, versions, and Fathers.

The symbol " . . . " marks the end of the discussion of one reading and the beginning of the next reading; sometimes a semi–colon is thus used (e.g., in Mark 9:6). If only a limited amount of evidence supports the second reading, the first reading may be given with no evidence cited. In such instances, a colon (:) follows the first reading (e.g., Mark 9:7).

Internal variation within a reading is indicated in parentheses: e.g., in Mark 9:6 Codex א, and Origen twice (*bis*), read απεκριθη instead of αποκριθη.

Tischendorf uses the abbreviations *et.*, *ita et.*, or *etc.* ("also," "so also," "and others") to indicate that the evidence for the reading is not being cited in full, but that certain witnesses are considered worthy of special mention (e.g., τ. προφητ., Matt. 1:22).

---

[2]See also the discussion in K. Lake, *The Text of the New Testament,* pp. 87–89, and A. T. Robertson, *Introduction to Textual Criticism of the New Testament,* pp. 55–64.

[3]In citing Griesbach, the following symbols are sometimes used to give additional information derived from Griesbach's own edition: Gb′, Griesbach prefers this reading; Gb″, Griesbach very much prefers this reading; Gb°, Griesbach has this reading in his text but does not prefer it; Gb°°, Griesbach very much disagrees with this reading of his text.

   b. Symbols Used. Since Tischendorf's edition was published prior to the establishment of the Gregory system of numeration, he sometimes uses symbols other than capital letters and
arabic numbers for uncial and minuscule manuscripts respectively. Any such additional symbols must be converted into the
proper Gregory number by referring to Gregory's volume or to
some other adequate key. In addition, outside the Gospels almost all arabic number designations must be converted. (See
Tischendorf, vol. 1, pp. ix–xxii, and vol. 2, pp. i–iii, for designations of principal MSS and versions.)

   A superscript *ev* (e.g., 49[ev]) designates a lectionary.

   Versions are indicated by non-capitalized abbreviations (see
Tischendorf, vol. 1, p. xxii). Subdivisions of versions may be indicated by superscript abbreviations. The following points are worthy
of special note: cop = Bohairic, syr[sch] = Peshitta, syr[p] = Palestinian Syriac, syr[hr] = both the Peshitta and the Harkleian Syriac.

   The symbol *stigma* (ϛ) indicates the Textus Receptus.

   An abbreviation indicating "others," "many others," "all others," etc. is often found in the citation of evidence. Such an
abbreviation refers to other witnesses of the kind immediately
preceding this abbreviation (e.g., other Greek MSS, other versions, or other Fathers). If, however, additional uncials are intended, this fact is indicated by the specific abbreviation *unc*
(e.g., unc[8] = eight additional uncials); while "others" following
either uncials, minuscules, or at the beginning of the evidence
refers to minuscules.

   If a word occurs twice in the same verse it may be indicated
in the apparatus as *pr* (the first occurrence), *sec* (the second
occurrence), etc.

   An extensive list of corrections of errors in the apparatus is
given in Tischendorf, vol. 3, pp. 1251–1302.

   For the meaning of some of the commonly used Latin terms,
see the Appendix of the present book.

   To illustrate the use of Tischendorf's critical apparatus by an
example, the data concerning the variant in Matt. 22:38 would
be read as follows:

Tischendorf's text, η μεγαλη και πρωτη, is supported by ℵ B, by the Greek text of the bilingual Codex D (but without the η before μεγαλη), L (but with η added before πρωτη), Z, eight minuscules, a lectionary, the Old Latin version (except two MSS), the Vulgate, Sahidic, Bohairic, Curetonian Syriac, Peshitta, Palestinian Syriac, Ethiopic, other unnamed versions, the Latin of one of Origen's works, Hilary, and a work by Augustine. The Textus Receptus reads πρωτη και μεγαλη with the support of Γ Δ 0107 (but the latter two read η before πρωτη) Π, nine other uncials, many minuscules, three Old Latin MSS, the Harkleian Syriac, the Armenian, one edition of the Persian, a work on ethics by Basil, and one other patristic writing.

9. Von Soden

a. Manner of Citation. Von Soden classifies his witnesses according to various groupings, a system upon which those of Merk and Bover are based. In the Gospels the principal groups are *H, I,* and *K* (see von Soden, vol. 2, pp. xiv ff.). *I* and *K* are further divided, the subgroups designated by Greek or English letters. For purposes of these groupings, von Soden divides the NT into three sections: Gospels, Apostle (Acts, Catholic Epistles, Pauline Epistles including Hebrews), and Revelation. As with Merk and Bover, if a MS is to be cited in only a part of a certain one of the groups a note to this effect is given accompanying the MS.

Since von Soden's system of MS notation is completely different from that of the other editors, it is necessary to convert each term into its Gregory equivalent. In his extensive description of MSS (vol. 1, pt. 1), von Soden gives the Tischendorf number followed by the Scrivener number for many MSS; but only in the Gospels is the Tischendorf number usually the same as the Gregory number. Gregory's *Griechischen Handschriften des NT* and Aland's *Kurzgefaßte Liste* give a cross-reference of MSS designations, but for extensive use of von Soden's apparatus the only satisfactory method is to use the small book by Benedikt Kraft, *Die Zeichen für die wichtigeren Handscriften des griechischen NT*, which lists von Soden's MSS, together with their Gregory equivalent, in the order in which von Soden gives them in his groupings. This latter point is important, because von Soden often cites a MS and follows it by *f*, *fff*, etc., indicating the one, two, three, or even four MSS which immediately follow in his groupings.

The observations concerning the manner of citation in Merk and Bover are generally applicable to von Soden's apparatus. In addition, von Soden often uses bold-face type to call attention to the fact that a reading in the apparatus is a change of form or of spelling from that of his text (e.g., Mark 1:10 ευθεως). Unlike Merk and Bover, von Soden always identifies the group in which each cited MS is found. For example, for the changed word order ταις ημ. εκ in Mark 1:9 he notes the *H* group and cites three MSS from this group (76f and δ 371); then he notes the *I* group and cites one MS from the α subgroup, one MS from the o subgroup, one MS from the π subgroup, etc. It is thus easier to locate MSS in von Soden's list than in Merk's.

Von Soden divides the variants in his critical apparatus into three sections, graded according to his opinion of their importance. Variants involving a bracketed portion of his text are always in the first section. This often means that the more significant aspect of a complex variant will be dealt with in the first or second section of the apparatus, while a more minor aspect of the same variant will be dealt with in the third section, with no cross-reference between the two. For example, in Mark 1:9 the second section of the apparatus indicates that D supports the changed word order υπο Ιω. εις τον Ιορδ., but the third section shows that D actually reads την, not τον.

b. Symbols Used. In von Soden's unique system of MSS notation, it is important to observe that a δ MS is always so designated in the apparatus (e.g., δ5 δ848). A MS with no letter preceding it is an ε MS in the Gospels, an α MS in Acts and the Epistles, etc. For example, in the Gospels δ1 is Codex B, 1 is ε1 (065), and 01 is ε01 ($\mathfrak{P}^1$).

Von Soden uses a relatively small number of symbols and abbreviations. Those which he regularly uses are the following:

a: (*ante*) before, in front of

p: (*post*) after, following

om: omit

gg: (*gegen*) against (i.e., the following evidence supports the reading opposite to the one previously referred to. This *gg* reading is usually von Soden's text.)

~: a change of word order

l: *(loco)* instead of

As in Merk and Bover, von Soden cites MSS in the order in which they appear in his groupings.

A hyphen (-) between two MSS merely indicates that they are assumed to be closely related textually in von Soden's groupings.

The abbreviation *exc* indicates an exception to what immediately precedes. For example, in Mark 1:2 ως . . . the *gg* reading is supported by the *Iη* group except for two MSS of this group; and it is supported by the *Iκ* group except for two MSS of the *a* subgroup *Iκa* and two MSS of the *b* subgroup *Iκb*. Careful attention must therefore be given to the precise location of the *exc*. For example, *Iφ*a exc . . . means that all of the *Iφ*a MSS except those indicated support the reading; on the other hand, *Iφ*exc a167 means that all of the *Iφ* MSS support the reading except one MS of the *a* subgroup.

Von Soden designates the Palestinian Syriac as *pa*. The abbreviation *af* indicates the African Latin of the Itala, which includes the MSS *k* and *e* in the Gospels and certain other MSS in other parts of the NT.

A bracketed citation of the Sinaitic and/or Curetonian Syriac should not be accepted, as these bracketed citations are apparently von Soden's suppositions and are not a part of the extant text of these versions.

A number given in large type in parentheses at the end of a variant—e.g., Mark 1:10 (1020 1449)—refers to a page or pages in vol. 1 of von Soden's work, where the variant is discussed or mentioned.

It is never safe to assume that any MS not specifically named by von Soden supports a given reading. If he cites a group or subgroup for a given reading, it is safe to assume only that the general consensus of these MSS support the reading. Any one or more MSS of the group may have a different reading which von Soden did not see fit to cite, or which will be found cited for a different reading; or one or more MSS may be lacking at this point, or von Soden may not have collated it for this chapter. Even when von Soden says that a given reading is supported by, for example, *I*o exc 129 it is still not sufficiently safe to say that every MS of this group specifically supports the reading. Note, for example, that von Soden indicates that he has collated *I*oε270 (Greg. 443) only cursorily in Matthew and Mark, which means that the readings of this MS cannot be taken for granted unless specifically cited.

The following typical examples may be helpful in learning to read variants as von Soden gives them:

Mark 1:2 ως 1 καθως (Luke 3:4) *K* gg *H* . . . (etc.) means that instead of the καθως of von Soden's text ως is supported by the *K* (Koinē) text, and this variant may have arisen under the influence of its occurrence in Luke 3:4. On the other hand (gg), von Soden's text, καθως, is supported by the *H* (Hesychian) text and by . . . (etc.).

Mark 1:3 του θ̅υ̅ ημων 1 αυτου (Jes. 40:3) . . . means that where von Soden's text reads αυτου, Tatian and a few other witnesses read του θεου ημων, the latter possibly having arisen under the influence of Isa. 40:3.

Mark 1:4 add ο a βαπτιζων (14 cf. Matt. 3:1) means that the witnesses cited add the article ο before the βαπτιζων of von Soden's text, under the influence of verse 14 of this chapter and possibly of Matt. 3:1.

Mark 1:5 εξεπορευοντο (with -ον- in bold-type face) means that the witnesses cited read εξεπορευοντο instead of the εξεπορευετο of von Soden's text.

Mark 1:9 ~ ταις ημ. εκ. (Matt. 3:1) means that the witnesses cited read ταις ημεραις εκειναις. instead of the εκειναις ταις ημεραις of von Soden's text, possibly under the influence of Matt. 3:1.

Mark 1:10 ευθεως *K* gg . . . means that the Koine text supports the spelling ευθεως against (*gg*) most of the Hesychian text which supports von Soden's text.

Mark 1:11 ηκουσθη1 εγεν.,~p ουρ. (etc.) means that where von Soden's text reads εγενετο three MSS of the *I* text substitute ηκουσθη and transpose this word so that it follows ουρανων (i.e., φωνη εκ των ουρανων ηκου.). In addition, the Old Latin MSS *a* and *f* support ηλθεν instead of εγενετο (without transposing the word order). Finally, some witnesses omit εγενετο without substituting any other word.

Finally, to illustrate by one complete example, the data concerning the variant in Matt. 22:38 would be read as follows:

> A change of word order, πρωτη και μεγαλη, in place of η μεγαλη και πρωτη of von Soden's text, is supported by the Koine text; it is supported also by the following MSS of the *I* text but with η before πρωτη: 2145, the MSS of the *I*π type and 273. Against this reading, von Soden's text is supported by Tatian, the MSS of the *H* text except for Δ and 1241, and by the following MSS of the *I* text: D (which however omits the η) Θ 700, the MSS of the *I*η type and the *I*ˡ type, and 1093; by the Palestinian Syriac, the Latin (Itala and Vulgate) except for two MSS of the Itala, and by the Syriac versions. Πρωτη alone is read by 1194. η μεγαλη alone is read by 27. In addition η is inserted before πρωτη by L 565 174 273 661.

9. Hoskier (Revelation only)

Hoskier lists and identifies all of the MSS of Revelation which were known to him, and he seeks to give the text of all. He does this by giving the text of the TR at the top of the page and giving the variants from the TR which are found in any of the MSS (and in some versions and Fathers). He indicates the MSS which are lacking for each verse. It may therefore be assumed that all MSS not cited among the variants from the TR and not cited as lacking the verse support the TR reading.

As mentioned previously, Hoskier cites the MSS by the Scrivener numbers, which must be converted into Gregory numbers. Hoskier furnishes a table of numbers for this purpose. However, in numerous instances he lists two Gregory numbers for a given Scrivener number, and sometimes he indicates doubt concerning the Gregory number. In such instances, the Gregory number must be determined from Gregory's volume, *Die griechischen Handschriften . . .* , or from some other source.

To illustrate by an example, in Rev. 1:5, where Hoskier's TR text reads λουσαντι, a corrector of one minuscule and the original hand of another minuscule read λουσας; a few other minuscules and some versions read ελουσεν; one minuscule is peculiarly written λοῦσαντι, λυσαντι is read by ℵ C A 𝔓¹⁸ and several minuscules; there is some support for λυσαντως, λυων, and ελυσεν; and the words και λουσαντι ημας are omitted by three minuscules.

B. THE SOLUTION OF SOME NEW TESTAMENT VARIANTS

1. The Procedure of Criticism

Before studying particular variants it will be well to state succinctly the principles and rules which should be followed, even though they have been discussed earlier to some extent (pp. 55–61, 72–75).

Determining the best reading in a variant involves both internal and external evidence. Internal evidence deals with the probabilities of what a scribe might have done, intentionally or unintentionally, that would have produced a different reading. External evidence deals with the MSS and other witnesses to the text in order to decide which reading has the best support by these witnesses. Either kind of evidence may be considered first, and ultimately both must be considered together. At the same time, there may be some advantage in considering internal evidence first, since it is more subjective; this prevents one's thinking from being unduly influenced initially by the evidence of the MSS.

a. Procedure for Deciding Internal Evidence. The following principles sometimes overlap; in other instances they may seem to contradict each other. The relative probabilities must be considered in reaching a conclusion.

In applying the following principles, refer to the types of errors discussed in chapter 4, pp. 55–61.

(1) *The reading from which the other reading(s) most likely arose* is probably original. This is the basic principle of internal evidence. The change or changes may have been due to any of the intentional or unintentional errors previously discussed.

This basic principle has several corollaries:

(a) The *harder* reading is often preferable. If a reading at first sight seems difficult to understand but on further study makes good sense, it is likely that a scribe intentionally or unintentionally changed the text to a reading that was easier to understand.

(b) The *shorter* reading is generally preferable if an *intentional change* has been made. The reason is that scribes at times made intentional additions to clarify a passage, but rarely made an intentional omission. Of course, this principle applies only to a difference in the number of words in the readings, not to the difference between a longer and a shorter word.

(c) The *longer* reading is often preferable if an *unintentional change* has been made. The reason is that scribes were more likely to omit a word or a phrase accidentally than to add accidentally.

(2) In variants where there is a parallel passage, such as in the Synoptic Gospels, a reading which is less verbally identical to the parallel is generally preferable. The reason is that scribes were more likely to change a reading to make it agree with the parallel than to make it disagree.

(3) A reading which is characterized by words and forms foreign to the author's style—that is, forms which he could have used but did not—is suspect.

   b. Examples to illustrate the principles of internal evidence. (In the examples, we will use uncial letters where their form is a possible factor.)

(1) The *explanatory* reading. In Col. 2:2 the author almost certainly wrote TON $\overline{\Theta\Upsilon}$ $\overline{X\Upsilon}$ ("[the mystery] of God, Christ"). However, this double genitive could have been misunderstood as "the mystery of the God of Christ," and the text shows how

scribes set about to re-word or clarify it with more than a dozen readings, such as omitting either "of God" or "Christ," or reading "of God and Christ," "of God the Father of Christ," and other variations. All of these other readings could have arisen from TON $\overline{\text{ΘY}}$ $\overline{\text{XY}}$, but this reading, if not others, could hardly have arisen from the other readings.

(a) The *harder* reading. In Mark 1:2 some MSS read "Isaiah the prophet"; others read "the prophets." In the quotation which follows, the first part is from Mal. 3:1; the second part is from Isa. 40:3. "Isaiah the prophet" is clearly the more difficult reading, which a scribe could easily have changed to the more strictly correct "the prophets." On the other hand, it is highly unlikely that a scribe would have changed "the prophets" to the single prophet, even if he knew that the second part of the quotation was from that prophet. The harder reading is therefore clearly to be preferred here.

(b) The *shorter* reading in an *intentional* change. In 1 Cor. 6:20, following the exhortation "Therefore glorify God in your body," some MSS add "and in your spirit, which are the Lord's." If this additional phrase was original, there would be no apparent reason for a scribe to omit it, for it is not inappropriate even though the preceding discussion dealt with the body. If it was not original, a pious scribe might have added it as an additional reminder. The shorter reading is therefore preferred, the longer reading doubtless being an intentional addition.

(c) The *longer* reading in an *unintentional* change. In 1 John 2:23 some MSS omit the second half of the verse, "he who acknowledges the Son has the Father also." The KJV italicizes this clause, indicating that these words were not in the Greek text from which the KJV was translated. It is possible that a later scribe added this clause to give the affirmative balance to the preceding negative statement. However, *both* clauses end with the same Greek phrase, TON $\overline{\text{ΠPᾺ}}$ ЄXЄI "has the Father." So it is probable that a scribe in copying this passage copied the first clause, then his eye skipped from the first TON $\overline{\text{ΠPᾺ}}$ ЄXЄI to the second, omitting the entire second clause.

(2) The *non-harmonized* or less identical parallel reading. The story of the rich young ruler is found in Matt. 19:16ff., Mark 10:17ff., and Luke 18:18ff. In Mark and Luke the young man asks, "*Good* teacher, what should I do . . . ?" and Jesus replies, "Why do you call me good?" In Matthew, some MSS agree with Mark and Luke, while others read, "Teacher, what *good thing* should I do . . . ?" and Jesus replies, "Why do you *ask* me *about what* is good?" If Matthew's original text was identical with that of Mark and Luke, there would have been no reason for a scribe to change it to a slightly different form. However, if Matthew's text originally differed from that of the other Gospels, a scribe could have changed it to make it agree with the others. Therefore the form which is not identical with the other Gospels is doubtless original.

(3) The *author's style*. This principle is largely limited to passages long enough to permit perception of the writer's style. For example, let us mention only one point in the discussion of the genuineness of Mark 16:9–20. In Mark 16:9 the first day of the week is called πρώτη "first." However, in Mark 16:2 and in all other instances of this phrase in the NT the word used is a form of μία "one"—i.e., "the (number) one day of the week."

   c. Procedure for Deciding External Evidence. The characteristics of the various text-types have been discussed in chapter 6, pp. 81–87. If the text-types are considered individually, the Alexandrian is generally the most reliable single text, although it sometimes contains a "learned" correction. At the same time, a reading which is supported by good representatives of two or more text-types may be preferable to a reading supported by one text-type exclusively. The reason for this is that if a reading has the support of good witnesses of several text-types it is more probable that the reading antedates the rise of the local texts instead of having originated in one of the local texts.

   The characteristics of the individual witnesses to a text-type must likewise be considered. Some witnesses are more consistently faithful to their text-type, while others are more corrupted by readings from other text-types or by peculiar readings. For example, although Codex ℵ is an Alexandrian MS it sometimes has Western readings and agrees with Codex D against the consensus of Alexandrian witnesses. Manuscripts from the fifth and later centuries, moreover, were almost always subject to being influenced by the Byzantine text and commonly have some Byzantine readings, even though they may be classified as witnesses to one of the other texts. If, therefore, the MSS of a given text-type are divided in their support, the true reading of a given text-type is more likely (1) the reading of the MSS which are generally most faithful to the text-type, (2) the reading which differs from that of the other text-types, (3) the reading which differs from that of the Byzantine text, and/or (4) the reading which is most characteristic of that text-type.

In deciding the MSS evidence for a variant, the support by text-types should be identified for each reading. Then it should be decided which reading has the best MSS support by text-types and/or parts of text-types. There will remain various witnesses whose text-type is not listed; these witnesses are often of significance, but the beginning student will probably not be able to make appreciable use of them. The discussions of the variants in the following pages omits this unclassified material for the present purpose, even though the presentation of the evidence is thereby somewhat oversimplified. This additional evidence can still, of course, be noted in the critical apparatuses for any use which the student can make of it.

The purpose of studying the external evidence is to decide which reading has the support of MSS and text-types that have been found to support more frequently the preferable readings. Against this evidence must be weighed the principles of internal evidence, and a final conclusion must take into account both lines of evidence. If the two are apparently contradictory, a satisfactory solution must be sought. To disregard external evidence and depend too completely upon internal evidence may lead to unduly subjective decisions. At the same time, one must not depend upon external evidence without proper regard to internal consideration, since no MS or text-type is perfectly trustworthy.

The text-type of many MSS and other witnesses is not known as yet. The tables on pp. 117–18 aim to list the principal witnesses whose text-type is fairly certain.

2. New Testament Examples

Most of the following evidence is found in the Bible Societies' Greek NT, with some additional evidence from Souter and other editors.

a. Luke 11:2. The first variant in Luke 11:2 has two readings: (1) πατερ only (L arm add ημων), and (2) πατερ ημων ο εν τοις ουρανοις.
Considering the internal evidence, which reading most likely gave rise to the other reading? This principle is important in the present variant. If the longer reading were original, there would be no apparent reason for its omission, as there is no difficulty of understanding or likelihood of accidental omission. On the other hand, if the shorter reading is original, a scribe could easily have added the words of the longer reading in order to harmonize this account of the Lord's Prayer with the account in Matthew and with the form of prayer which was commonly used in worship. Thus Reading 2 could have developed from Reading 1, but the reverse is unlikely. Reading 1 is therefore preferable on this principle.

The harder reading is generally preferable. In the present variant there seems to be nothing in either reading which would impress a scribe as being difficult of interpretation; either "Father" alone or the longer phrase would easily be understood as referring to God. The principle of the harder reading is therefore probably not significant in the present variant.

Reading 1 is the shorter reading. If, therefore, the variant has been an intentional one, Reading 1 is more likely the original. That the variant is indeed intentional is indicated by the fact that the parallel account of the Lord's Prayer (Matt. 6:9)

	GOSPELS	ACTS
Alexandrian	𝔓1 𝔓3 𝔓4 𝔓5 𝔓7 𝔓22 𝔓39 (𝔓66) 𝔓75 ℵ B C L Q T (W Lk. 1–8:12 Jn.) (X) Z (Δ Mk.) Ξ (Ψ exc. Mt.) 054 059 060 0162 20 33 164 215 376 (579 exc. Mt.) 718 850 892 1241 (1342 Mk.) Boh (Sah) Ath Clem-Alex Cyr-Alex (Or)	𝔓8 𝔓45 (𝔓50) ℵ Λ B (C) Ψ 048 076 096 6 33 81 104 326 1175 Boh (Sah) Ath Cyr-Alex Clem-Alex? (Or)
Caesarean	𝔓37 𝔓45 Θ (W Mk. 5:31ff.) N O Σ Φ Fam 1 Fam 13 28 157 565 700 1071 1604 Geo Arm Pal-Syr Eus Cyr-Jer (Or)	(Text-type not determined in Acts)
Western	𝔓25 D (W Mk. 1–5:30) 0171 It, esp. k e Sin-Syr Cur-Syr Tert Ir Clem-Alex Cyp (Aug) Diatessaron?	𝔓29 𝔓38 𝔓41 𝔓48 D E 066 257 383 440 614 913 1108 1245 1518 1611 1739 2138 2298 It Hark-Syr mg
Byzantine	A E F G H K M P S U V (W Mt., Lk. 8:12ff.) Y (Δ exc. Mk.) Γ Π Ω Most minuscules Goth Later versions Later Fathers	H L S P 049 Most minuscules Goth Later versions Later Fathers

Figure 5

	CATHOLIC EPISTLES	PAUL, HEBREWS	REVELATION
Alexandrian	$\mathfrak{P}^{20}$ $\mathfrak{P}^{23}$ $\mathfrak{P}^{72}$ $\mathfrak{P}^{74(?)}$	$\mathfrak{P}^{10}$ $\mathfrak{P}^{13}$ $\mathfrak{P}^{15}$ $\mathfrak{P}^{16}$ $\mathfrak{P}^{27}$ $\mathfrak{P}^{32}$ $\mathfrak{P}^{40}$ $\mathfrak{P}^{46}$ $\mathfrak{P}^{65}$	$\mathfrak{P}^{18}$ $\mathfrak{P}^{24}$ ($\mathfrak{P}^{47}$)
	ℵ A B (C) P Ψ	ℵ A B (C) H I M P Ψ	(ℵ) A (C) P
	048 056 0142 0156	048 081 088 0220	0207 0169
	33 81 104 323 326 424c 1175 1739 2298	6 33 81 104 326 424c 1175 1739 1908	61 69 94 241 254 1006 1175 1611 1841 1852 2040 2053 2344 2351
	Boh (Sah)	Boh (Sah)	
	Ath Cyr-Alex Clem-Alex? (Or)		
Western	$\mathfrak{P}^{38}$		
	D E	D E F G	F?
	383	88 181 383 915 917 1836 1898 1912	
	It Hark-Syr mg	It	It?
	Ir Tert Cyp Aug Eph		
Byzantine	H K L S	K L 049	046 051 052
	42 398		82 93 429 469 808 920 2048
	Most other minuscules	Most other minuscules	Most other minuscules
	Goth Later versions	Goth Later versions	Goth Later versions
	Later Fathers	Later Fathers	Later Fathers

Figure 6

(Caesarean text not determined for these sections of NT)

Note: A *corrector* of a MS must be treated as a separate MS, and its text-type must be separately determined.

reads πατερ ημων ο εν τοις ουρανοις with no variant; a scribe could intentionally, or even unintentionally, have added the words from Matthew in Luke, since that of Matthew was probably the more familiar form of the prayer. Moreover, there does not seem to be any basis upon which the longer reading, if original, could have been changed unintentionally to the shorter reading by homoioteleuton, etc. Reading 1, then, is preferable as the shorter reading.

The reading which is characteristic of the author is preferable. A check of Moulton and Geden's concordance indicates that Luke quotes Jesus as addressing God as "Father" in direct address five or six times without a possessive or other attributive qualifier, and not at all with such modifiers. Moreover, while Luke contains numerous references to God as Father, in various cases, only one has a modifier referring to heaven, and it is different from the present variant (Luke 11:13, ο πατηρ ο εξ ουρανου). Thus Reading 1 appears to be the reading which is more characteristic of the author.

The external evidence is as follows:

	Alex.	Caes.	West.	Byz.
(1) πατερ	𝔓75 ℵ B L (Or) Cyr-Alex	f¹ 700 arm (Or)	syˢ Tert	
(2) πατερ ημων ο εν τοις ουρανοις	C Ψ 1241 (sa) bo (Or)	Θ f¹³ 28 157 geo 565 892 1071	D it syᶜ	Λ K P Δ Π Byz

Reading 1 is the reading of the strongest part of the Alexandrian text, part of the Caesarean, and a small part of the Western. Reading 2 is the reading of part of the Alexandrian, a stronger part of the Casarean, and the reading of the Western and Byzantine texts. Reading 1 is therefore favored, since it is supported by the best part of the Alexandrian plus some additional support. Although Reading 2 has some support from all four text-types, its support includes the Byzantine, which often has harmonized readings. Thus Reading 1 is slightly favored by external evidence. Reading 1 is therefore accepted, since it is strongly favored by internal evidence and slightly by external evidence.

Comparing the conclusions of internal and external evidence, the reading πατερ is preferable in each case. The editors of the critical texts agree with this conclusion, while the TR, of course, follows the longer (Byzantine) reading.

b. Luke 24:53. The three principal readings for this variant are (1) ευλογουντες only, (2) αινουντες only, and (3) αινουντες και ευλογουντες. Considering internal evidence, Reading 3 could have given rise to Reading 2 by homoioteleuton but not to Reading 1. Reading 1, however, could have been changed to 2 as being more appropriate in reference to God, and 3 could have developed by conflation of 1 and 2. Reading 1 is thus preferable as the reading which best explains the origin of the others.

As for the harder reading, both of the participles in this variant are used in the NT in reference to God, as a concordance will show. At the same time, ευλογέω is more commonly used of blessing people, and the Epistle to the Hebrews uses the argument that the inferior person is blessed by the superior. A scribe might therefore have intentionally changed ευλογουντες to αινουντες as a more appropriate word. The principle of the harder reading may therefore point to Reading 1 as against 2, but probably would have no bearing upon Reading 3.

If an intentional change has occurred, Reading 1 or 2 would be preferable to 3. If an accidental change occurred, 3 could have been shortened to 2 but could hardly account for 1. This principle, therefore, is not decisive here.

As for the characteristic of the author, six of the eight occurrences of αἰνέω (aside from the present passage) in the NT are found in Luke and Acts, always in reference to God. Luke–Acts also contain more than one-third of the NT instances of εὐλογέω, although only two aside from the present passage speak of blessing God. Thus both words are common in Luke, with εὐλογέω more frequent but with αἰνέω more common in reference to God. Thus αἰνέω may be termed somewhat more characteristic of the author, but no strong conclusion is warranted, since Luke uses both words in reference to God.

Reading 1 is therefore acceptable by three of the four principles of internal evidence, Reading 2 by two principles, and Reading 3 by two (although by one of these only tacitly). At the same time, the only principle which discriminates between all three readings points rather definitely to Reading 1 as original. Internal evidence thus seems to favor ευλογουντες as the original, with αινουντες as a possible alternative choice.

External evidence gives the following witnesses:

	Alex.	Caes.	West.	Byz.
(1) ευλογουντες	$\mathfrak{P}^{75}$ ℵ B C* L (sa) bo	sy^{pal} geo	sy^s	
(2) αινουντες			D it (Aug)	
(2) αινουντες και ευλογουντες	(X) 33 892 1241	Θ f^1 f^{13} 28 157 565 700 1071 arm		A K W Δ Π Byz

The MSS evidence is here rather clearly defined as to text-types, with Reading 1 being the reading of most of the Alexandrian text, with a small amount of support from the Caesarean and Western; Reading 2 is the reading of the Western text; and Reading 3 is the reading of the Caesarean and Byzantine texts, with some Alexandrian support.

Reading 1, then, is supported by the best single text-type. One characteristic of the Western text is to paraphrase, and Reading 2 may easily be a paraphrase of 1 (as was previously suggested on the basis of internal evidence). Conflation is likewise a characteristic of the Byzantine text, and Reading 3 may easily be a conflation of 1 and 2 (as was also suggested on the basis of internal evidence). Since the Caesarean text sometimes agrees with the Alexandrian and sometimes with the Western, in this instance the combination of both influences may have produced the conflate reading of the Caesarean. Another possibility is that all of the Caesarean witnesses listed here, except the Palestinian Syriac, have been influenced by the Byzantine text. At any rate, the Caesarean text here is hardly to be preferred over the other readings. Thus external evidence strongly supports Reading 1, with 2 a paraphrase of 1, and 3 a conflation of 1 and 2.

Since external evidence clearly supports Reading 1 and internal evidence supports 1 more strongly than 2, it seems clear that the original text is ευλογουντες. Most editors agree with this conclusion, although Tischendorf reads αινουντες, Vogels and the TR read αινουντες και ευλογουντες, and Merk indicates his doubt by reading [αινουντες και] ευλογουντες.

c. John 1:18. For our purposes, in this variant we will discuss only the readings θεός and υἱός, which would be written $\overline{\Theta C}$ and $\overline{\Upsilon C}$ respectively, thus differing by only one letter.

The reading from which the other most likely arose is surely θεός, primarily because it is also clearly the harder reading, referring to Jesus as "only-begotten God" as compared with the much easier "only-begotten Son." Yet "God" is acceptable, since a few verses earlier (1:1) Jesus is called God. This reading is even surer when we see that the best text does not include a definite article before μονογενής; so the reference is to Christ's nature as deity— "the only-begotten, who himself is deity, has set forth God."

There is no issue, of course, of a shorter or longer reading, unless we consider the very minor reading which omits both "God" and "Son"; and there is no parallel passage which could involve harmonization.

As for the characteristic of the author, John reads μονογενής alone once and μονογενής υἱός twice, but μονογενής θεός not at all elsewhere. Of course, these examples are too limited in number to warrant strong conclusions. It should be noted, moreover, that John does use θεός in reference to Christ, and that the meaning of μονογενής is "only," "only one of its kind," or "unique," and does not refer to birth as such. All three readings are therefore consistent with Johannine usage.

Internal evidence therefore strongly supports θεός as the reading most likely to give rise to the other, since it is the harder reading.

The external evidence is as follows:

	Alex.	Caes.	West.	Byz.
(1) θεος	$\mathfrak{P}^{66}$ $\mathfrak{P}^{75}$ ℵ B C* L 33 850 (sa) bo (Or) Cyr-Alex	geo² (Or)	Cl Ir	
(2) υιος	Wsupp (X) Ψ 892 1241 (sa) Ath	Θ f¹ f¹³ 28 157 565 700 1071 sypal arm geo¹ Eus	it syc Cl Ir Tert	A K Γ Δ Λ Π Byz

Remember that church fathers often quote a passage more than once and sometimes in different forms, thus attesting to more than one reading, as Clement and Irenaeus do here.

Reading 1 is supported by the best part of the Alexandrian text; Reading 2 is supported by a minor part of the Alexandrian and by the other three texts. Reading 1 is thus supported by the best single text-type but has hardly any other support. This suggests that it may be merely an Alexandrian correction. We would be more inclined to accept an Alexandrian reading with at least some support from other non-Byzantine texts. However, Reading 1 is supported by $\mathfrak{P}^{66}$, the earliest extant witness to this passsage, as well as $\mathfrak{P}^{75}$. With the present support, if Reading 1 appeared to be a grammatical correction or a scholarly improvement of the text it might well be rejected against the weight of the other text-types; but θεος does not seem to be a reading of this sort. When the internal evidence is considered together with the external evidence, the picture seems understandable. It appears that Reading 1, the harder reading, was changed to the easier Reading 2 by most other witnesses (and omitted by a few), with only the Alexandrian text resisting the change to the easier reading. Reading 1 may therefore be accepted against the combined evidence of the other text-types because of its strong support from internal evidence. Merk, Vogels, Nestle, BFBS, and WH read θεος, while Tischendorf, Bover, and von Soden follow the TR in reading υιος.

d. 1 John 3:1. A different type of variant is found in 1 John 3:1, in which the alternatives are (1) the inclusion and (2) the omission of the words και εσμεν.

If the change were an intentional one, preference for the shorter reading would point to the omission. On this basis, a scribe might have added the words to strengthen the statement and make positive what was only implicit without the addition. On the other hand, if the longer reading were original the shorter reading could have come by accidental omission from homoioteleuton; written in uncials and with no division of word the context would appear as follows:

ΤΕΚΝΑΟΥ̅ΚΛΗΘΩΜΕΝΚΑΙΕϹΜΕΝΑΙΑ

And a scribe could easily have passed over και εσμεν because of its similarity to κληθωμεν.

Either reading might have given rise to the other. If these words were not original, they might have been added intentionally, to strengthen the sense. If they were included originally, they might have been omitted accidentally by homoioteleuton. Both readings are easy to understand, so neither is a hard reading. Internal evidence is therefore not decisive for this variant.

Here is the external evidence:

	Alex.	West.	Byz.
(1) και εσμεν	𝔓74 ℵ A B C P Ψ 33 81 323 424ᶜ 1175 2298 (sa) bo	itᵖᵗ Aug	
(2) omit	056 326 1175	itᵖᵗ	K L Byz

Reading 1 is Alexandrian and Western (no Caesarean text has been identified outside the Gospels). Reading 2 is Byzantine. Reading 1 is therefore clearly preferred on external evidence, especially since a reading with only Byzantine support is usually suspect.

Since internal evidence is noncommittal and external evidence strongly supports Reading 1, we conclude that the author included και εσμεν, and that these two words were omitted accidentally. All of the critical editors include these words, while the TR omits them.

   e. Mark 8:26. The variant at the end of Mark 8:26 is somewhat different from the preceding ones. There are four principal readings, with some additional internal variations. These readings are as follows:

> (1) μηδε εις την κωμην εισελθης
> (2) μηδε εις την κωμην εισελθης μηδε ειπης τινι εν τη κωμη
> (3) υπαγε εις τον οικον σου και μηδενι ειπης εις την κωμην
> (4) υπαγε εις τον οικον σου και εαν εις την κωμην εισελθης
>   μηδενι ειπης (μηδε) εν τη κωμη

Reading 1 can most nearly account for the others. Reading 2 may then be an expansion of 1 to explain why the man was not to enter the village; 3 may be a new approach, making explicit the command implied earlier in the verse that the man was to go home, and giving a slightly different reference to the village; and 4 may be an expansion of 3 attempting to explain why the man needed to be admonished not to speak to anyone in the village when he was commanded to go home. On the other hand, if 2 or 3 is original it is difficult to account for the simpler 1; and 4 is clearly an attempt to make an easier reading.

   The principle of the harder reading likewise seems not to be very helpful. Readings 1 and 2 are probably harder in the context, since Mark tells us that "Jesus sent him to his house, saying, . . . " but only Readings 3 and 4 quote Jesus as actually telling him to go home.

   Reading 1 is the shortest reading, of which Reading 2 might be an intentional expansion; Reading 4 might be an intentional expansion of 3; but 3 is hardly a mere intentional expansion of 1. Accidental omission from the longer to the shorter readings seems unlikely.

In three similar passages in Mark, Jesus orders the healed person not to speak of what has happened. In the present variant, Reading 1 is the only reading which does *not* contain this admonition. This might suggest that 1 is least characteristic of the author. On the other hand, 1 and 2 seem more characteristic of the general style used in Mark than are 3 and 4.

Internal evidence is therefore not strongly conclusive, but Reading 1 may be favored to some extent.

We now turn to external evidence. The student should for the present consider only the four readings listed above and pass over the others, which have only limited support.

	Alex.	Caes.	West.	Byz.
Reading 1	ℵ B L sa bo[pt]	W f[1] geo[pt]	sy[s]	
Reading 2	C (X) Δ 33 579 892 1241 1342 bo[pt]	118 157 700 1071		A E F G H K M S U V Y Γ Δ Π Ω Byz goth
Reading 3			D it[pt]	
Reading 4		Θ Φ 565 f[13] 28 arm geo[pt]		

Reading 1 is supported by a strong part of the Alexandrian text, part of the Caesarean, and one Western witness. Reading 2 is supported by part of the Alexandrian, some Caesarean witnesses, and clearly the Byzantine. Reading 3 is probably the Western reading. Reading 4 is supported by good Caesarean witnesses and is probably the Caesarean reading since it stands almost alone. Reading 1 and 2 thus have the best MSS support, and Reading 1 is probably to be preferred because its Alexandrian witnesses are superior to the Alexandrian witnesses of 2 and because it has better support from the other non-Byzantine texts. Moreover, the fact that 2 is clearly the Byzantine reading makes 2 less likely the original reading, since both the Alexandrian and Caesarean support for 2 is weaker than their support for 1.

Returning now to the internal evidence, in the light of the external evidence the picture seems clearer. From the general characteristics of the text-types, it seems reasonable to conclude that Reading 1 is original—i.e., Jesus "sent him to his house, saying, 'Do not even enter the village.' " The Western text, which often paraphrases, reworked the passage (Reading 3) so as to quote Jesus as telling the man to go home, adding "and speak to no one in the village" instead of "do not enter the village." The Byzantine text (which then influenced some Alexandrian and Caesarean MSS) took Reading 1 and combined it with the latter part of 3, thus giving a partially conflated reading. The Caesarean text (Reading 4), which often supports either the Alexandrian or the Western, is divided, with some of its witnesses supporting the Alexandrian and others developing the Western reading into a weaker and easier reading. We therefore conclude that Mark originally wrote that Jesus told the man to go home and not to enter the village; Mark merely stated the first part of this and quoted Jesus for the second part. The editors agree in this reading (Reading 1), while the TR has the Byzantine reading (Reading 2).

f. Luke 15:21. The variant in Luke 15:21 which we shall discuss has two readings: (1) the addition and (2) the omission of the words ποίησόν με ὡς ἕνα τῶν μισθίων σου at the end of the verse.

The reading which seems best able to explain the development of the other reading is the omission (Reading 2). In verse 19 the son states that he intends to tell his father, "Make me as one of your hired servants." If these words were in the original text of verse 21 as well, there would be no reason for a scribe to omit them intentionally (the assumption that a scribe omitted them either because he did not think it necessary to repeat them again, or because he felt that the father must have interrupted the son before his speech was completed, would be more appropriate to a deliberate editor than to a mere copyist). On the other hand, if this clause were not original here the scribe could easily have added it, either under the unconscious influence of verse 19 or intentionally on the basis that if Jesus said that the son intended to say these added words he must in fact have said them and the Gospel should include them.

Neither reading seems to be a "hard" reading. If there were no variant present, there would seem to be no difficulty in accepting either reading. The longer reading could be justified as carrying out what the son had said he would tell his father. The shorter reading could be justified either on the grounds that the father interrupted the son before he finished his speech or because the realization of his father's love and forgiveness made the humiliating request obviously inappropriate.

The shorter reading is, of course, Reading 2; and if the change in the text is intentional, the shorter reading is preferable. On the other hand, since σου occurs both just before and at the end of the additional words there is a possibility that the longer reading is original and that the omission has occurred accidentally by homoioteleuton; but with only one identical syllable involved this seems to be a less likely possibility.

The question of the reading which is more characteristic of the author is more difficult to answer. The Gospel could be examined to see whether any similar situations occur, but it is not likely that there are enough to warrant a clear conclusion.

The external evidence is as follows:

	Alex.	Caes.	West.	Byz.
(1) ποιησον με ως ενα των μισθιων σου	ℵ B (X) 33 1241	700 1071	D	U
(2) omit	𝔓[75] L Q Δ Ψ 892 sa bo	N Θ f[1] f[13] 28 157 565 1071 sy[pal] geo arm	it sy[c.s] (Aug)	A K P Γ Δ Λ Π Ω goth Byz

Reading 1 is supported by a slighter stronger part of the Alexandrian text and by the principal uncial MS of the Western text. Reading 2 is supported by a slightly weaker part of the Alexandrian, by the Caesarean and Byzantine, and by a good part of the Western text. Although the combination of Alexandrian witnesses supporting Reading 1 is generally reliable, the good Alexandrian witnesses supporting Reading 2 plus the distribution of support from all four text-types make it difficult to decide which reading is preferable on the basis of external evidence.

This variant, then, will have to be decided on the basis of internal evidence, which favors Reading 2 as the reading from which the other reading most likely developed, and as the shorter reading where an intentional addition was made.

g. Other Variants. The preceding discussions of variants should help the student to see how to follow the principles through to the solution of a textual problem. There are, of course, a host of other variants which could have been discussed with equal profit for this purpose, plus a multitude in which the principles do not seem to point clearly to one reading or another. For further practice, the student might profitably make an analysis of some such variants as the following:

John 3:15, εν αυτῷ, where ἐν seems to be the correct preposition and the phrase is intended to modify ἔχῃ, while all of the alternatives are easier readings modifying πιστεύων, and εἰς αὐτόν is also a harmonization with 3:16.

Mark 1:1, in which υιου θεου may be an intentional addition, but which is more likely original and was accidentally omitted because of the string of similar letters in the phrase "gospel of Jesus Christ Son of God"—ΕΥΑΓΓΕΛΙΟΥ‾ΙΥ̅‾ΧΥ̅‾ΥΥ̅‾ΘΥ̅.

Matthew 6:1 (not in UBS text; see Nestle-Aland), in which δικαιοσυνην is apparently original and was changed to agree with ελεημοσυνην by a scribe who failed to understand that 6:1 was a general statement covering more than verses 1–4.

Romans 5:1 εχομεν / εχωμεν, in which either reading may be the result of an error of hearing; or the force of εχωμεν, if original, may have been misunderstood and changed to the indicative; but εχομεν seems to suit better the sense of the verses following.

Second Corinthians 7:14 (see Nestle-Aland), in which επι Τιτου may be original, with the article ἡ inserted by a scribe to make it clear that the phrase modifies καύχησις rather than the verb, while the change of preposition is a characteristic Western paraphrase.

Revelation 1:5, in which λυσαντι is probably original and was changed to the easier λουσαντι either intentionally or accidentally.

John 7:53–8:11, which is not only omitted by good MSS evidence but which is written in a style and vocabulary quite different from that of the Gospel generally.

Mark 16:9–20, omitted by fewer MSS, but the omission is clearly supported by internal evidence, including the fact that the style and vocabulary are radically different from that of the rest of Mark.

John 5:3–4, which may be an instance of an explanatory note originally written in the margin and later mistakenly incorporated into the text. The Greek is unlike John's style.

First John 5:7–8, in which the addition concerning the three heavenly witnesses, although incorporated into the TR, has virtually no Greek support and is clearly a late addition.

Acts 12:25, a difficult variant in which the critical apparatuses of some editors contain errors. Contrary to several editors and versions, the correct reading may be εἰς, whose uncial form, ∊IC, could have been mistaken by a scribe as the more easily understood ἐκ, (cf. ∊IC / ∊K) which he then "corrected" to ἐξ, since it was followed by a vowel. The passage with εἰς will mean "they returned to Jerusalem to fulfill their ministry," the aorist participle here being perfectly analogous to Acts 25:13, "they arrived in Caesarea to greet Festus."

Other variants which may be suggested, either because of the importance of the passage, the support of text-types, or the internal evidence, include the following:

Matt. 6:4, 6, 18 εν τω φανερω
Mark 6:20 ηπορει / εποιει
Mark 6:22 αυτης της / αυτου / etc., a tantalizing variant

Luke 23:45
Luke 24:6, a Western omission or "non-interpolation"
Luke 24:12
John 8:34 της αμαρτιας
John 14:2 οτι
Acts 3:11, a Western paraphrase
Rom. 7:25 χαρις τω θεω, et al.
2 Cor. 1:12 αγιοτητι / απλοτητι
Eph. 1:1 εν Εφεσω
Phil. 2:5 τουτο φρονειτε, et al., a difficult passage
1 Tim. 3:16 ος / θεος / ὅ
Heb. 8:8 αυτους / αυτοις
1 John 4:20

In addition, there are numerous variants which the student
may profitably examine which involve harmonization of parallel passages in the Synoptic Gospels (e.g., the story of the rich
young ruler), parallels between Ephesians and Colossians, and
the quotation of OT passages in the NT.

A different type of exercise is that found in a few passages
such as Mark 6:33 (προηλθον αυτους, etc.) and Col. 2:2 (του
θεου χριστου, etc.). Here the student may attempt to determine
the manner in which the eight or ten variant readings arose,
and to determine which is the original reading.

In James 4:13–14, which includes several variants, the student may trace a number of the principal witnesses through
these two verses and observe that hardly any two of the principal witnesses agree completely throughout this passage.

Chapter 8

COLLATION AND CLASSIFICATION OF MANUSCRIPTS

A. REASONS FOR COLLATING

The process of comparing one text or MS with another is collation. In textual criticism, collation commonly refers to the process of comparing a MS with a generally available printed text and recording the differences. In this way the full text of the new MS is readily available without printing its entire text; one need only read the printed text against which the MS was collated and substitute the collated differences. In this way the full text of MSS may be kept on file in much less space than would be required for the full printed text of the MSS, and in addition the distinctive elements of each MS are in this way more easily noted.

A second reason for collating a MS is to add its testimony to the critical apparatus of a printed text. In this case, the best procedure is to collate the MS against the text in whose critical apparatus it is to be used.

A third reason for collating a MS is to analyze its textual affinities—i.e., to determine with which other witnesses it generally agrees—and to determine, if possible, its text-type. Theoretically, this could be done by checking every substantial variant in the entire MS. Commonly, however, the MS is collated against the TR and the variations from the TR are analyzed. Since the

TR is (generally) Byzantine in text-type, the resulting collation will reveal non-Byzantine readings of the MS. Whether the amount of these differences from the TR is large or small will indicate whether the MS is primarily Byzantine or non-Byzantine. The variants from the TR can then be analyzed to determine with which witnesses the MS most often agrees; and, if possible, with which text-type it may be identified.

Another method sometimes used to determine the textual character of a MS is to study each variant in which three or more readings occur regardless of whether the MS agrees or disagrees with the TR at these points. The discussion of the present chapter, however, is based on a consideration of variants from the TR.

In addition to an analysis of the variants of the MS from the TR to determine the textual character of the MS, it will often be helpful to analyze the substantial variants which the MS does *not* follow, since a visible contrast is thus established between the textual character of the variants which are found in the MS and those which are not found.

B. The Method of Recording a Collation

A collation should always include the name of the text against which the MS was collated, including the specific edition: e.g., "the University of Chicago reprint of the 1873 Oxford edition of the TR," "the 1953 Macmillan reprint of the Westcott-Hort text."

In recording a collation, the name of the NT book should be given at the top of each page of the collation. The chapter and verse should then be given with each separate entry in the collation.

The first reading must *in every instance* be the reading of the printed text against which the MS is being collated. This reading is followed by a mark of separation, such as a square bracket (]), then the reading of the MS. The collation is then read as follows: "In chapter ———, verse ———, where the printed text reads ———, the MS which is being collated reads ———."

No unnecessary words should be included in the collation. For example, if the printed text reads ἐν οἴκῳ and the MS reads ἐν τῷ οἴκῳ, the collation should read simply "εν] add τῳ," or else "εν] εν τῳ." If the variant concerns a word or phrase which appears in exactly the same form more than once in the verse, a small superscript numeral following the word or phrase indicates which occurrence of the word is intended: e.g., και².

If two or more successive words differ from the collating base, they should be recorded together as one variant if they are logically associated (e.g., εν αυτῳ] εις αυτον), but should be recorded separately if they could occur independently of one another.

For the sake of illustration, the following is a collation of one page of the Nestle 25th edition, using TR (University of Chicago reprint of the Oxford 1873 edition) as the collating base. By comparing this collation with these printed texts (or, for all practical purposes, by comparing it with almost any of the more recent editions of the Nestle text and almost any edition of the TR), the student may see how various differences have been collated and recorded. For the present purpose, the page of the Nestle-Aland text will be presumed to be a one-page fragment of a manuscript.

LUKE

18:14 inc. o¹
18:15 επετιμησαν] επετιμων
18:16¹ προσκαλεσαμενος αυτα ειπεν] προσεκαλεσατο αυτα λεγων
18:17 εαν] αν
18:18² επηρωτησε] επηρωτησεν
18:19 ειπε] ειπεν

---

¹ (The superscript 1 following "o" indicates that the page begins with the first occurrence of o in the verse; the superscript 1 following the reference 18:16 is a footnote reference.) Two differences are involved in this variant in 18:16, but they are recorded together because they are interrelated.

² For some purposes, differences of ν-movable need not be collated. If there is any doubt, however, it is safer to collate them. The 2 following σου in 18:20 (following page) means that this is the second occurrence of σου in this verse.

18:20 σου²¹ omit

18:21 ειπε] ειπεν

18:21 εφυλαξαμην] εφυλαξα

18:21 μου] omit

18:22 ταυτα] omit

18:22³ ουρανω] τοις ουρανοις

18:23 εγενετο] εγενηθη

18:24⁴ περιλυπον γενομενον] omit

18:24 ειπε] ειπεν

18:24⁵ εισελευσονται εις την βασιλειαν του θεου] εις την
    βασιλειαν του θεου εισπορευονται

18:25 εστι] εστιν

18:25⁶ τρυμαλιας] τρηματος

18:25⁶ ραφιδος] βελονης

18:26 ειπον] ειπαν

18:27 ειπε] ειπεν

18:27 εστι παρα τω θεω] παρα τω θεω εστιν

18:28 ειπε] ειπεν

18:28⁷ expl. ημεις

---

³Both a changed form of the noun and the addition of the article are combined in this note since the two items are interrelated. On the other hand, if the TR had read ουρανοις here as does Nestle, and the only change involved the article, the collation would have been recorded as "εν] add τοις" or else "εν] εν τοις." Here the breathing is written over the ἑν because the word ἑν appears earlier in the verse; without the aspiration this note could have been indicated as εν².

If a variant involves an addition, it is generally better for the sake of consistency to give the word from the collating base which *precedes* the addition, even if the added word is more closely related to the word which *follows* it: e.g., "εν] add τοις," rather than "ουρανοις] τοις ουρανοις."

⁴These two words are interrelated and are therefore noted together. It is unlikely that a MS would include the one word without including the other.

⁵This variant involves both the transposition of the verb and a different word for the verb. If there were other textual complications involved, or if the transposition were still farther removed, it might be better to record this as two separate variants, as follows: "εισελευσονται] omit," and then "θεου] add εισπορευονται."

⁶These two variants are listed separately, although the words are adjacent to each other, because they are not dependent upon each other and could occur separately.

If any words or letters in the MS being collated are missing or illegible, square brackets are used to indicate these unread portions; e.g., ερχ[ ]αι. If there is no doubt of what the missing letters are, the letters may be included within the brackets; e.g., ερχ[ετ]αι. If letters are only partially legible and therefore uncertain, but are partially visible, the letters may be written but a dot should be placed under each doubtful letter; e.g., ερχεται.

Abbreviations, symbols, etc., in a MS should be read as if they were spelled out fully, and they therefore do not need to be noted in a collation if this spelling agrees with that of the collating base. An exception is the *nomen sacrum* δ̄ᾱδ̄, which can represent any of the three or more common spellings of "David." This abbreviation must therefore be recorded as an abbreviation, to show that it cannot be assumed to support a particular spelling.

If the MS contains a correction, both readings should be recorded: e.g., "υποτασσεσθαι]υποτασσεσθαι, corrected above the line to υποτασσεσθε"; or, "του] omitted by first hand but added in the margin."

A special word must be said with reference to collating a lectionary. A lection almost always begins with one of six set phrases (see pp. 35–36). In addition, the opening words of the biblical passage immediately following this introductory phrase may often be slightly accommodated to the lectionary form. These changes should be noted as a part of the introduction to the lection and not as a textual variant. For example, the TR of Luke 20:19 begins, καὶ ἐζήτησαν οἱ ἀρχιερεῖς καὶ οἱ γραμματεῖς ἐπιβαλεῖν ἐπ᾽ αὐτὸν τὰς χεῖρας, while certain lectionaries read τῷ καιρῷ ἐκείνῳ ἐζήτουν οἱ ἀρχιερεῖς καὶ οἱ γραμματεῖς ἐπιβαλεῖν ἐπὶ τὸν Ῑν τὰς χεῖρας. The beginning of this lection should be collated as follows: "Inc. I[8] εζητουν οι αρχιερεις και

---

[7]If the page had ended in the middle of the next word, this would have been recorded in the collation as "expl. αφεν[τες]." Similarly, if the page had begun in the middle of a word the note would have read, e.g., "18:14 inc. [ταπει]νωθησεται."

[8]"Inc. I" refers to the first in the list of phrases beginning a lectionary passage (see p. 36).

οι γραμματεις επιβαλειν επι τον Ιησουν τας," which brings the text of the lectionary to the point at which it joins the regular NT text.

C. The Use of Collations

In addition to recording the differences between a MS and a given printed text so as to make known the full text of the MS, a collation serves as a basis for analyzing the textual affinities of the MS and determining its text-type. For this purpose, the collated differences (e.g., differences from the TR) are listed with the various witnesses which agree with these readings, and the results are summarized.

In order to determine the textual affinities, one should observe what text-type(s) support each reading, when a reading is supported by one text-type, when it is supported by more than one, etc. The summary should then show both the frequency with which each individual text-type supports the readings of the MS and also the frequency of support by combinations of text-types. For example, for a part of a certain witness such a summary is as follows:

Total Support by Individual Text-types
(in any combination)

Alexandrian	13 times
Caesarean	22 times
Western	7 times
No type	7 times

Support by Particular Combinations of Text-types

Alexandrian-Caesarean	9	Alexandrian-Caesarean-Western	2
Caesarean alone	8	Alexandrian-Western	1
Caesarean-Western	3	Western	1
Alexandrian alone	1	No text-type	7

This summary indicates that the witness under study is definitely of a Caesarean text-type, with a closer secondary relationship to the Alexandrian than to the Western text.

In addition, the relationship of the MS to particular individual MSS or witnesses should be noted, in order to determine to which witness *within* the text-type the MS is most closely related. It must be observed, however, that the relationship of a MS to a *text-type* cannot be determined from its relationship to individual witnesses. For example, the Caesarean witness referred to above is supported by ℵ and B as frequently as by any Caesarean MS. Such a situation may occur because no individual witness is a perfect representative of its text-type; any witness may have peculiar readings, a certain amount of Byzantine readings, occasional readings from other text-types, etc. Hence, the determination of the relationship of a MS to a *text-type* must come from its agreement with the consensus of the witnesses to that text-type, which is a standard to which no single witness to the text-type is likely to measure up.

Finally, if one wishes to discern as clearly as possible the textual affinity of a MS, the inquirer should study the variants that do *not* agree with the MS and determine the text-type of these variants as well. This will furnish a contrast which should help to confirm the text-type of the MS in question. Thus in the case of the Caesarean witness referred to above, the variants which this witness did *not* read were primarily strong Alexandrian readings and unique Western readings. A study of these opposing variants has an additional value: if, for example, a MS is characterized by Alexandrian readings in its variants from the TR, but it is found that there is an appreciable number of Alexandrian readings among the variants which the MS does not read, it will then be seen that the MS is not a thoroughly Alexandrian witness, but has a partially Byzantine character.

Determination and analysis of these opposing variants is particularly important in the examination of the text of a church father. Since the texts of patristic quotations of the NT are naturally fragmentary, one cannot merely assume either (1) that the

Father follows fully the text-type with which his variants are identified, or (2) that his text is Byzantine wherever it is not cited in support of another text-type. In many passages no text at all will be available. Therefore, while an analysis of the Father's quotations will reveal the text-type of his text, an analysis of the opposing quotations is necessary to determine whether he follows this text-type fully or whether there is an appreciable element of this text-type which his text does not follow.

In conclusion, it may be said that the collation of the text of a witness, while requiring meticulous attention to detail, can be both personally rewarding and a significant contribution to textual scholarship.

APPENDIX: SOME COMMONLY USED LATIN TERMS AND THEIR MEANING†

add., addit, addunt: adds, add
al.: other(s)
al pc: a few others (witnesses of the same kind as those
    immediately preceding)
al[60] *fere:* nearly sixty others
al vix mu: not a great many others
al sat mu: a significant number of others
al pl: very many others
al certe pl: certainly very many others
al longe pl: very many others by far
al fere omn: nearly all others
al omn: all others
ad: at, to
aliq.: other (i.e., in some other form)
alt.: the other (e.g., a second occurrence)
ante: before, in front of
ap., apud: with, according to; *codd. ap. Or:* codices known to Origen
aut: or
bis: twice
c., cum: with (i.e., supported by)
cet., cett.: another, the others, others

---

†The plural of a word written in Latin abbreviation is indicated by doubling the final letter of the abbreviation (e.g., *ed., edd.; cet, cett.; ms., mss.; p., pp.*).

cf.: compare
comm.: commentary
comma: phrase
coniung., conjung.: joined together
cor., corr.: corrector, corrected
def.: is lacking
e, ex: from (source)
e.g.: for example
ed., edd.: editor, editors
enim: for, because
err.: error
et., etiam: also
exc.: except
fere: almost
fin.: the end
fluct: varies (*lectio non fluct:* the reading does not vary)
fort., fortasse: perhaps, probably
hab., habent: has, have
i.e.: that is
id., idem: the same
infra: below
int., interp.: interpretation (e.g., the Latin translation of the work)
ita: so, thus
item: thus
leg.: it reads, they read
loc., loco: place(s), location(s) (e.g., in this place, in place of)
mal., malunt: badly, they express it badly
mg.: margin
mu., mult.: many
non: not
nonnull.: some, several
om.: omit
omn.: all
opt.: the best
patr.: Fathers, patristic writings
pauc., pc.: a few
pl., pler.: very many
plane: completely
plur.: most
plus: more
pm.: many

pon.: place, put
post: after, following
postea: afterwards
pr.: first occurrence
pr., praem.: precede(s) (i.e., a reading which precedes)
praeterea: furthermore, besides
punct.: punctuation
rel, rell.: remaining (i.e., the remaining witnesses)
saec.: century
saep., saepe: often
schol.: scholium, scholia, marginal comment(s)
sec.: the second occurrence (e.g., της sec.)
sec., secundum: according to (e.g., sec. Matt.)
sed: but
sem.: once only
seq.: the next following
sic: thus (sometimes used to indicate that a MS reads thus, even
        though its reading may seem strange)
sim.: similar, similarly
sine: without, not including
sive . . . sive: either . . . or
solum: alone
supp., suppl.: supply, supplement
supra: above, previous
tant., tantum: only so much (i.e., not including any added words)
tert.: third
tot.: the whole
text: text (e.g., as opposed to a marginal reading or to an
        accompanying commentary)
u., v.: verse
uel, vel: or
uers., vers.: version
uid., vid.: it seems, apparently
uide, vide: see
usque, usque ad: up to, as far as
ut: as
ut uid., ut vid., ut vdtr.: as it seems; *minusc ut vid pauc:* a few
        minuscules apparently (support this reading)
utroq., utroque: both

SUPPLEMENTARY READINGS[†]

CHAPTER 1

Bruce, *Are the N. T. Documents Reliable?*, ii, 14–20.
Colwell, *Study*, ii, 38–45.
Kenyon, *Handbook*, i, 1–7.
Metzger, "Recently Published Greek Papyri," 26.
Parvis and Wikgren, i, 1–5.
Souter, i, 3–5.
Vaganay, 9–13.
Westcott and Hort, 1–11.

CHAPTER 2

Diringer, *Alphabet*, 457–61.
*Diringer, *Hand-Produced Book*, i, 13–52; iv, 125–66; v, 170–72, 190–95, 203–33.
Gregory, *Canon and Text*, Part 2, i–ii, 314–28.
Hatch, *Facsimiles and Descriptions*, 3–21.
*Hatch, *Principal Uncial Mss.*, 3–25.
Kenyon, *Handbook*, ii, 19–41.
Kenyon, *Our Bible*, i, 9–15.
*Kenyon, *Story*, iii, 20–37.
*Metzger, *Text*, i, 3–21.
Price, xi, 156–58.
Roberts, C. H., "The Christian Book."
Roberts, C. H., "The Codex."
Robertson, iii, 41–54.

[†]More significant readings are indicated with an asterisk (*).

Souter, i, 5–9.
*Thompson, i–xii, 1–171.

CHAPTER 3

A. *Greek* MSS
Baikie, i, iii, xi–xiii, 13–23, 36–37, 50–60, 225–58, 271–320.
Diringer, *Hand-Produced Book*, v, 195–202.
Gregory, *Canon and Text*, Part 2, iii–v, 329–93.
*Hatch, *Principal Uncial Mss.*
*Hatch, *Minuscule Mss.*
Herklots, vii–viii, 81–108.
*Kenyon, *Bible and Archaeology*, ix–x, 204–59.
*Kenyon, *Handbook*, ii, 41–44; iii–iv, 45–144.
Kenyon, *Our Bible*, vii, 124–54.
*Kenyon, *Story*, vii, 71–80; viii, 98–107; ix, 108–26; Appendix 1, 145–49.
*Lake, ii, 11–23.
*Metzger, *Text*, ii, 36–37.
Moulton, i–iii, 11–77.
Nestle, ii, 28–40, 53–93.
Parvis and Wikgren, i, 1–24; vii, 125–36.
Price, xii, 161–76.
Robertson, iii, 52–54; v, 70–96.
Scrivener, vol. 1: iii, 71–89; iv–xiv, 90–418.
Souter, iii, 19–32.
Streeter, ii, 47–50.
Taylor, iii–v, 8–26.
Tischendorf, 15–32.
Twilley, v, 37–41; vi, 46–49.
Vaganay, i, 21–35.

B. *Versions*
Bruce, xv–xvii, 181–208.
Goodspeed
Gregory, *Canon and Text*, Part 2, vi, 394–418.
Herklots, iv–vi, 41–80.
*Kenyon, *Handbook*, v, 145–241.
Kenyon, *Our Bible*, viii, 155–77.
*Lake, iii, 24–48.
*Metzger, ii, 67–86.
Nestle, ii, 93–144.
Nida, v, 74–81.
*Parvis and Wikgren, ii, 25–68,
*Price, xiii–xiv, 177–201.

Robertson, vi, 102–30.
Scrivener, vol. 2, i–iv, 1–166.
Souter, iv–vi, 33–75.
Taylor, vi, 27–38.
Twilley, v, 38–40; vi, 45.
*Vööbus (entire book)

C. *Patristic quotations*
Altaner (entire book)
Bardenhewer (entire book)
*Greenlee, ii–iii, 15–28.
Gregory, *Canon and Text*, Part 2, vii, 419–36.
*Kenyon, *Textual Criticism*, ii, 19–44; vi, 242–64.
*Lake, iv, 49–53.
*Metzger, *Text*, ii, 86–89.
Milligan, i, 2–32.
Nestle, ii, 144–55.
Robertson, vii, 131–47.
Scrivener, vol. 2, vi, 167–74.
Souter, vii, 76–93.
Streeter, ii, 45–47.
Taylor, vii, 39–43.

CHAPTER 4

Colwell, ii, 45–64.
Gregory, *Canon and Text*, part, x, 480–508.
*Kenyon, *Our Bible*, vi, 98–103.
*Kilpatrick
Lake, i, 3–6.
*Metzger, *Text*, vii, 186–206.
Robertson, vii, 150–60.
Streeter, ii, 35–45; Appendix 1, 565–71.
Twilley, vi, 42–44.

CHAPTER 5

Gregory, *Canon and Text*, Part 2, viii, 437–66.
*Kenyon, *Handbook*, vii, 265–313; viii, 314–69.
Kenyon, *Our Bible*, vi, 100–104, 109–18, 119–23.
*Kenyon, *Story*, iv, 41–46.
*Lake, v, 62–86.
*Metzger, *Text*, iii–iv, 95–129.
Nestle, i, 1–27.

*Price, xv, 202–11; xvi, 212–20.
Taylor, viii, 44–48.

CHAPTER 6

Greenlee, i, 10–14.
Kenyon, *Handbook*, iii, 52–55; vii, 295–306; viii, 363–69.
*Kenyon, *Story*, vii, 82–84; viii, 98–107.
*Lake, v–vi, 67–86, 89–90.
Lake, Blake, and New (entire article)
Metzger, *Chapters*, i, ii, iv, 1–72, 97–120.
*Metzger, *Text*, iv, 129–45; vi, 161–63, 169–73.
*Metzger, *JBL* 64.
*Price, xv–xvi, 205–20.
Streeter, vii–xii, 64–69, 77–108, 572–81, 598–600.
Taylor, ix–xi, 49–75.
Westcott-Hort (entire book)

CHAPTER 7

A. How to Read a Critical Apparatus
Lake, App. A-B, 87–95.
Robertson, vii, 55–64.
See the introductions to the various critical editions of the N.T. for
    notes on the use of each.

B. The Solution of Some NT Variants
Colwell, *JBL* 66,2.
Kenyon, *Our Bible*, App. 1, 247–56.
*Metzger, *Text*, vi, 175–79; viii, 207–46.
Robertson, viii–xiii, 160–220 (but takes no account of develop-
    ments since W-H)
Streeter, iv, 86–89, 97–98; v, 115–16; vi, 136–38, 143–44.
Taylor, xii, 76–107.
Twilley, vii, 53–63.
Vaganay, v, 193–205.
Zuntz (entire book)
See also the articles listed in Metzger, *Bibliography*, vii, 103–15.
Consult the critical commentaries for notes on variants in
    particular passages.

CHAPTER 8

Greenlee, ii–viii, 15–100.
*Metzger, *Text*, vi, 179–81.
Lake, Blake, and New (entire article)

SELECTED BIBLIOGRAPHY

Aland, Kurt. *Kurzgefaßte Liste der griechischen Handschriften des Neuen Testaments. Arbeiten zur neutestamentlichen Textforschung, Band 1.* Berlin: Walter de Gruyter, 1963.

Aland, Kurt, and Barbara Aland. *The Text of the New Testament: An Introduction to the Critical Editions and to the Theory and Practice of Modern Textual Criticism.* Translated by Errol F. Rhodes. 2d ed., revised and enlarged. Grand Rapids: Eerdmans, 1989.

Altaner, Berthold. *Patrology* (English translation by Hilda C. Graef). Freiburg: Herder, 1960.

Baikie, James. *Egyptian Papyri and Papyrus Hunting.* London: The Religious Tract Society, 1925.

Bardenhewer, Otto. *Patrology* (English translation by Thomas J. Shahan). Freiburg, Herder, 1908.

Beegle, Dewey M.. *God's Word Into English.* New York: Harper, 1960.

Bruce, Frederick Fyvie. *Are the New Testament Documents Reliable?* 3d ed. Chicago: Inter-Varsity Christian Fellowship, 1950.

_____. *The Books and the Parchments.* London: Pickering and Inglis, 1950.

Colwell, Ernest Cadman. *The Study of the Bible.* Chicago: The University of Chicago Press, 1937.

_____. "Genealogical Method: Its Achievements and Limitations." *Journal of Biblical Literature* 66,2 (June 1947).

Diringer, David. *The Alphabet.* London: Hutchinson's Scientific and Technical Publications, 1953.

_____. *The Hand-Produced Book.* London: Hutchinson's Scientific and Technical Publications, 1953.

Duplacy, Jean. *Où en est la Critique Textuelle du Nouveau Testament?* Paris: Gabalda, 1959.

Ehrman, Bart D. *The Orthodox Corruption of Scripture: The Effect of Early Christological Controversies on the Text of the New Testament.* New York: Oxford University Press, 1993.

Elliott, J. K. *A Bibliography of Greek New Testament Manuscripts,* with Foreword by Bruce M. Metzger. Cambridge: Cambridge University Press, 1989.

Goodspeed, Edgar J. "The Versions of the N.T." *Interpretation* 3, 1 (Jan. 1949), pp. 62–67.

Greenlee, J. Harold. *The Gospel Text of Cyril of Jerusalem. Studies and Documents XVII.* Edited by Silva Lake and Carsten Høeg. Copenhagen: Ejnar Munksgaard, 1955.

Gregory, Caspar René. *Canon and Text of the New Testament.* Edinburgh: T. & T. Clark, 1907.

_____. *Textkritik des Neuen Testamentes[sic].* 3 vols. Leipzig: Hinrichs, 1900–1909.

Hatch, William Henry Paine. *The Principal Uncial Manuscripts of the New Testament.* Chicago: University of Chicago Press, 1939.

_____. *Facsimiles and Descriptions of Minuscule Manuscripts of the New Testament.* Cambridge, Mass.: Harvard University Press, 1951.

Herklots, H. G. G. *How Our Bible Came to Us* (published in England as *Back to the Bible*). New York: Oxford University Press, 1954.

Kenyon, Frederic George. *Handbook to the Textual Criticism of the New Testament.* 2d ed. London: Macmillan, 1926.

_____. *Recent Developments in Textual Criticism.* Oxford: Oxford University Press, 1933.

_____. *Our Bible and the Ancient Manuscripts.* 5th ed. Revised by A. W. Adams. New York: Harper, 1958.

_____. *The Bible and Archaeology.* New York: Harper, 1940.

Kilpatrick, George Dunbar. "The Transmission of the New Testament and its Reliability." *Proceedings of the Victoria Institute.* Vol. 89. Reprinted in *The Bible Translator* 9, 3 (July 1958), pp. 127–36.

Lake, Kirsopp, Robert P. Blake, and Silva New. "The Caesarean Text of the Gospel of Mark." *Harvard Theological Review* 21 (1928), pp. 206–404.

_____. *The Text of the New Testament,* 6th ed. Revised by Silva New. London: Rivingtons, 1943.

Metzger, Bruce M. *Annotated Bibliography of the Textual Criticism of the New Testament. Studies and Documents XVI.* Edited by Silva Lake and Carsten Høeg. Copenhagen: Ejnar Munksgaard, 1955.

_____. *Chapters in the History of New Testament Textual Criticism.* *New Testament Tools and Studies.* Vol. 4. Grand Rapids: Eerdmans, 1963.

_____. *The Text of the New Testament: Its Transmission, Corruption, and Restoration.* 3d enlarged ed. New York: Oxford University Press, 1992.

_____. "The Caesarean Text of the Gospels." *Journal of Biblical Literature* 64 (Dec. 1945), pp. 457–89.

_____. *Manuscripts of the Greek Bible: An Introduction to Greek Palaeography.* New York: Oxford University Press, 1981.

_____. "Recently Published Greek Papyri of the New Testament." *Biblical Archaeologist* 10, 2 (May 1947), pp. 26–44.

_____. "Recent Spanish Contributions to the Textual Criticism of the N.T." *Journal of Biblical Literature* 66, 4 (Dec. 1947), 401–27.

_____. *A Textual Commentary on the Greek New Testament,* 2d ed. *A Companion Volume to the United Bible Societies' Greek New Testament (Fourth Revised Edition).* Stuttgart: Deutsche Bibelgesellschaft, and United Bible Societies, 1994.

Milligan, George. *The New Testament Documents.* London: Macmillan, 1913.

Moulton, James H. *From Egyptian Rubbish Heaps.* London: C. H. Kelly, 1916.

Nestle, Eberhard. *Introduction to the Textual Criticism of the Greek New Testament* (English translation by William Edie). London: Williams and Norgate, 1901.

Nida, Eugene A. *God's Word in Man's Language.* New York: Harper, 1952.

Parvis, Merrill M., and Allen P. Wikgren. *New Testament Manuscript Studies.* Chicago: University of Chicago Press, 1950.

Pickering, Wilbur N. *The Identity of the New Testament Text.* 2d ed. Nashville: Thomas Nelson, 1980.

Price, Ira Maurice. *The Ancestry of Our English Bible.* 3d ed. Revised by William A. Irwin and Allen P. Wikgren. New York: Harper, 1956.

Roberts, Colin H. "The Christian Book and the Greek Papyri." *Journal of Theological Studies* 50, 199–200 (July-Oct. 1949), pp. 155–68.

_____. "The Codex." *Proceedings of the British Academy* 40 (1954), pp. 169–204.

Robertson, Archibald Thomas. *An Introduction to the Textual Criticism of the New Testament.* Nashville: Sunday School Board of the Southern Baptist Convention, 1925.

Scrivener, Frederick Henry Ambrose. *A Plain Introduction to the Criticism of the New Testament.* Edited by Edward Miller. 4th ed. 2 vols. London: George Bell and Sons, 1894.

Souter, Alexander. *The Text and Canon of the New Testament.* Revised by C. S. C. Williams. Naperville, Ill.: Alec R. Allenson, 1954.

Streeter, Burnett Hillman. *The Four Gospels: A Study of Origins.* London: Macmillan, 1951.

Taylor, Vincent. *The Text of the New Testament.* New York: St. Martin's, 1961.

Thompson, Edward Maunde. *An Introduction to Greek and Latin Palaeography.* Oxford: Clarendon Press, 1912.

Twilley, Leslie Douglas. *The Origin and Transmission of the New Testament.* Grand Rapids: Eerdmans, 1957.

Vaganay, Leo. *An Introduction to the Textual Criticism of the New Testament,* 2d ed. Revised and updated by Christian-Bernard Amphoux; English translation by Jenny Heimerdinger. Cambridge: Cambridge University Press, 1991.

Vööbus, Arthur. *Early Versions of the New Testament. Papers of the Estonian Theological Society in Exile 6.* Stockholm, 1954.

Westcott, Brooke Foss, and Fenton John Anthony Hort. *Introduction to the New Testament in the Original Greek, With Notes on Selected Readings.* Reprinted, Peabody, Mass.: Hendrickson, 1988.

_____. *The New Testament in the Original Greek. Introduction and Appendix.* New York: Harper, 1882.

Zuntz, Günther. *The Text of the Epistles: A Disquisition upon the Corpus Paulinum.* London: The British Academy, 1953.

MODERN EDITIONS OF THE GREEK NEW TESTAMENT WITH CRITICAL APPARATUS

A. Large editions

Tischendorf, Constantinus. *Novum Testamentum Graece,* editio octava critica major. Vol. 1, 1869; Vol. 2, 1872. Leipzig: Giesecke and Devrient. Vol. 3, *Prolegomena.* Edited by Caspar René Gregory. Leipzig: Hinrichs, 1894.

von Soden, Hermann. *Die Schriften des Neuen Testaments in ihrer ältesten erreichbaren Textgestalt.* Vol. 1, 1902–10; vol. 2, 1913. Göttingen: Vandenhoeck & Ruprecht.

Hoskier, Herman C. *Concerning the Text of the Apocalypse.* 2 vols. London: Bernard Quaritch, 1929.

Legg, S. C. E. *Novum Testamentum Graece. Evangelium Secundum Marcum*, 1935. *Evangelium Secundum Matthaeum*, 1940. Oxford: University Press.

_____. *The New Testament in Greek: III. The Gospel According to St. Luke.* Edited by The American and British Committee of The International Greek New Testament Project. Part One, Chapters 1–12 (Oxford: Clarendon Press, 1984). Part Two, Chapters 13–24 (Oxford: Clarendon Press, 1987). This is in some sense a continuation of S. C. E. Legg's editions of Matthew and Mark.

B. Small Editions

Souter, Alexander. *Novum Testamentum Graece*, rev. ed. Oxford: Clarendon Press, 1947.

Vogels, Heinrich Joseph. *Novum Testamentum Graece et Latine.* 4th ed. Freiburg and Barcelona: Herder, 1955.

Kilpatrick, George D., ed. Ἡ Καινὴ Διαθήκη. 2d ed. London: British and Foreign Bible Society, 1958.

Bover, José M. *Novi Testamenti Biblia Graeca et Latine.* 6th ed. Revised by José O'Callaghan. Madrid: Consejo Superior de Investigaciones Cientificas Patronato "R. Lulio"—Instituto "Fr. Suarez," 1981.

Merk, Augustinus. *Novum Testamentum Graece et Latine.* 10th ed. Rome: Pontificio Instituto Biblico, 1984.

Aland, Barbara and Kurt, eds. *Novum Testamentum Graece.* 27th ed. Stuttgart: Deutsche Bibelgesellschaft, 1993.

The Greek New Testament. 4th revised edition. Edited by Barbara Aland, Kurt Aland, Johannes Karavidopoulos, et al. New York: United Bible Societies, 1993.

Hodges, Zane C., and Arthur L. Farstad, eds. *The Greek New Testament According to the Majority Text.* Nashville: Thomas Nelson, 1982.

INDEX OF PERSONS AND SUBJECTS

INDEX OF SCRIPTURE REFERENCES†

†Passages discussed in some detail are indicated with an asterisk (*).